FRIEDRICH HAYEK

FRIEDRICH HAYEK

The **ideas** and **influence** of the **libertarian economist**

EAMONN BUTLER

Hh

HARRIMAN HOUSE LTD

3A Penns Road
Petersfield
Hampshire
GU32 2EW
GREAT BRITAIN

Tel: +44 (0)1730 233870
Fax: +44 (0)1730 233880
Email: enquiries@harriman-house.com
Website: www.harriman-house.com

First published in Great Britain in 2012

ISBN: 9780857191755

British Library Cataloguing in Publication Data
A CIP catalogue record for this book can be obtained from the British Library.

Published in association with the Institute of Economic Affairs. The mission of the Institute of Economic Affairs is to improve understanding of the fundamental institutions of a free society by analysing and expounding the role of markets in solving economic and social problems.

Set in Minion and Gotham Narrow.

Printed and bound in the UK by CPI Group (UK) Ltd, Croydon, CR0 4YY.

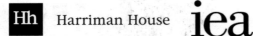

CONTENTS

Get the eBook for free

As a buyer of the printed book of *Friedrich Hayek*, you can download the full eBook free of charge.

Simply point your smartphone or tablet camera at this QR code or go to: **ebooks.harriman-house.com/hayek**

CONTENTS

ABOUT THE AUTHOR

DR EAMONN BUTLER is director of the Adam Smith Institute, a London-based think tank dealing in market economic policy. He has an MA in Economics and Psychology from the University of St Andrews, and a PhD in Philosophy from St Andrews.

Dr Butler's most recent books include *The Best Book on the Market* (Capstone, 2008), *Milton Friedman* (Harriman House, 2011), *Adam Smith: A Primer* (Institute of Economic Affairs, 2007) and *Rotten State of Britain* (Gibson Square, 2009).

Earlier books include *Ludwig von Mises: Fountainhead Of The Modern Microeconomics Revolution* (Gower, 1988) and *Forty Centuries of Wage and Price Controls* (co-authored with Robert L. Schuettinger, Green Hill Publishers, 1979). With Dr Madsen Pirie, he is also author of a number of popular books on IQ published by Pan. Since 1979 he has co-authored and edited a number of publications on economic and policy issues for the Adam Smith Institute.

Dr Butler writes regularly on economics for leading newspapers. In 2012 he received an Honorary D.Litt from Heriot-Watt University.

ABOUT THE AUTHOR

INTRODUCTION

What this book is about

THIS BOOK IS A straightforward guide to the ideas and
influence of the Nobel economist Friedrich Hayek (1899–
1992), regarded by many as the twentieth century's most
important thinker on social and economic freedom.

An Austrian who fled Nazi oppression, Hayek's insights into the
workings of the free society and free economy, and his critique of
socialism that stemmed from them, helped shatter the postwar
faith in economic planning, and were a significant influence on
world leaders such as Ronald Reagan and Margaret Thatcher. His
ideas continue to influence economists, political scientists,
politicians and students across the world today.

Hayek received the 1974 Nobel Prize in Economic Sciences,
largely for his early work explaining the cause and effect of boom-
bust cycles such as that of the 1920s and 1930s. He also made
significant contributions in the fields of legal theory, psychology
and information science. But Hayek remains best known for his
work in political science, and for his books *The Road to Serfdom*
(a caustic analysis of how socialism, if consistently followed,
develops into totalitarianism) and *The Constitution of Liberty* (a
major exposition of the foundations and principles of a free
society).

Perhaps Hayek's key insight is the ability of market economies, through the price system, to process a vast amount of information – including dispersed and personal information that no central planner could even know, let alone manage. This enabled him to explain the vibrancy of free, 'spontaneous' social order, in contrast to the drab failure of planned societies.

Who this book is for

This book is written for people who want to learn more about the case for individual freedom and free-market capitalism – and the deeply insightful case for liberalism put forward by one of its greatest exponents. (Throughout this book, 'liberalism' is used in the European sense of support for individual freedom and limited government.)

The book explains Hayek's ideas on the nature of society and economics, and some of the criticisms that have been made of them. It aims to do so in plain language and without distortion. So there are no distracting academic-style footnotes or bibliography – just an essential reading list of Hayek's main writings and important books about him.

The book should interest school and college students of economics, politics and social science, giving them a concise introduction to some radical ideas that are too frequently ignored by teachers and textbooks. Students will find plenty here with which to challenge those teachers!

Hayek is also relevant politically, as one of the leading gurus behind the rise of the New Right in the 1980s and 1990s. His ideas had a huge influence on a growing band of academics, intellectuals, think-tankers and politicians; and through them, these ideas influenced the radical pro-freedom and pro-capitalism agendas of Margaret Thatcher in Britain, Ronald Reagan in America, and other world leaders, including many from the former Soviet-bloc countries.

Why this book was written

At a conference in London in the early 1980s, the writings of F. A. Hayek were being discussed. The Alternative Bookshop had brought along a selection of Hayek's books; but I could see that many of the people browsing through them were intimidated by the academic density of some of these works and did not know where to start. Hayek was one of my main intellectual inspirations – I knew him slightly and met him often at conferences – and I was familiar with his ideas. So I resolved to write a short book on those ideas to help others discover and understand them.

That book was published in 1983, and was well received by many people who had never been introduced to Hayek's ideas, or even to the arguments for liberalism and capitalism. However, the book is now difficult to obtain; and increasingly, I have come to see its shortcomings. It is too long, too technical and too detailed for such a primer. It was also written when Hayek was still alive and working, which meant that I could not take a detached view of his output, nor fully assess his more enduring impact, nor take account of the many useful criticisms of his work that have been made subsequently.

This book, by contrast, is short and focused; the language is non-technical; it avoids academic trappings; it assesses the longer-term impact of Hayek's contribution and reviews the main arguments of his critics and defenders. So I hope it should provide an ideal primer on its subject.

How this book is structured

The book starts by showing Hayek's importance in the development of free-market and liberal ideas, and his impact on economic and social policy debates during his lifetime and today.

Chapter 2 outlines Hayek's groundbreaking ideas on the structure of society, and how societies do not have to be consciously planned in order to work efficiently. Chapter 3 explores the role of freedom and the law in maintaining the harmony of such societies.

Chapter 4 takes this idea into economics, sketching Hayek's view of markets as hugely effective at processing the dispersed and patchy information on which economic life is based – far more so than any central planner. Chapter 5 goes on to describe Hayek's view on boom and bust cycles, and his analysis of how inept government policies distort the market process and stop it from working.

Chapter 6 explains Hayek's argument that much current economic thinking is just a particular case of how the methods of the physical sciences are misapplied to social issues, for which they are unsuited – leading to major policy mistakes.

One of those policy mistakes, according to Hayek, is the doctrine of socialism and central planning. Chapter 7 outlines Hayek's critique of socialism, and Chapter 8 his critique of the idea of 'social justice'.

Chapter 9 sets out the constitutional and institutional framework that Hayek believes would promote the operation of a free and prosperous society, before the short conclusion that is Chapter 10.

A TIMELINE OF F. A. HAYEK'S LIFE AND WORK

1899	Friedrich August von Hayek born into an academic family in Vienna, capital of the Austro-Hungarian Empire.
1917	During the first world war, Hayek joins the Austro-Hungarian Army, serving in artillery and in aircraft on the Italian front.
1919	Austria abolishes the minor aristocratic 'von' titles. Throughout his career, Hayek styles himself simply as 'F. A. Hayek'.
1920	Hayek works for brain scientist Constantin Monakow, stimulating his thoughts on perception and knowledge.
1921	Hayek earns a doctorate in law from the University of Vienna. At Vienna he discovers the work of the 'Austrian School' economists.
1921	Leading Austrian School economist Ludwig von Mises hires Hayek to help in an office dealing with postwar finance issues.

1922   Living through Weimar Germany's hyperinflation makes Hayek critically aware of the dangers of inflation.

1923   Hayek earns another doctorate from Vienna, in political science.

1923–4   Hayek becomes a research assistant at New York University.

1927   Mises and Hayek found the Austrian Institute for Business Cycle Research. On the basis of this work, Hayek publishes *Monetary Theory and the Trade Cycle* (1929), *Prices and Production* (1931) and *The Pure Theory of Capital* (1941).

1928   Hayek first meets John Maynard (later Lord) Keynes at a conference in London.

1931   Hayek moves to the London School of Economics at the invitation of British economist Lionel (later Lord) Robbins.

1931–2   Hayek becomes the leading critic of Keynes, writing critical reviews of his books and exchanging letters in *The Times* on the merits of government spending versus private investment.

1936   Keynes publishes *The General Theory of Employment, Interest and Money*. Though alarmed at its inflationary implications, Hayek neglects to review the work, which becomes hugely influential.

1936   At the London Economic Club, Hayek gives a talk on the key role of information in economic life, a theme he would continue to refine.

1938   After Germany's Anschluss with Austria, and fearing Nazi persecution if he returns home, Hayek becomes a British citizen.

1944   Evacuated to Cambridge during the second world war, Hayek publishes *The Road to Serfdom*. It becomes an international success.

1944   Hayek is elected to the prestigious British Academy.

1945–6   Hayek lectures across the United States and becomes Visiting Professor at Stanford University.

1947   Hayek founds the Mont Pelerin Society, aiming to keep liberty alive in a hostile postwar world. The first meeting, in Switzerland, is attended by Mises, the philosopher Karl (later Sir Karl) Popper, the historian C. V. (later Dame Veronica) Wedgwood, the young economists (both later Nobel laureates) Milton Friedman and George Stigler, and many other leading thinkers.

1950   Hayek joins the Committee on Social Thought at the University of Chicago. He publishes a study on scientific method, *The Counter-Revolution of Science* (1952) and another on the nature of the mind and perception, *The Sensory Order* (1952).

1953	Chicago economist Milton Friedman and others participate in Hayek's regular seminars on the philosophy of science.
1956	Businessman and former fighter pilot Antony (later Sir Antony) Fisher founds the free-market Institute of Economic Affairs, having been inspired by a conversation with Hayek in 1946.
1960	Publication of *The Constitution of Liberty*, Hayek's major statement of the foundations and principles of a free society.
1962	Hayek moves to the University of Freiburg, West Germany. His ideas on unplanned orders and other subjects are published in *Studies in Philosophy, Politics and Economics* (1967). He begins work on another major book, *Law, Legislation and Liberty*.
1972	As prices soar in Europe and the US, Hayek publishes a passionate critique of inflation and the Keynesian policies that cause it in *A Tiger by the Tail*. He goes on to propose solutions in *Choice in Currency* (1976) and *The Denationalisation of Money* (1976).
1973	With the death of Mises, Hayek becomes the leading living member of the Austrian School of Economics.
1974	Hayek is awarded the Nobel Memorial Prize in Economic Sciences for his early work on business cycles. His Nobel Lecture chides economists and social scientists on their 'pretence of knowledge'.
1975	Through an introduction by the Institute of Economic Affairs, the British Conservative leader Margaret Thatcher meets Hayek for the first time, and is greatly impressed.
1984	Hayek is appointed a Companion of Honour.
1988	Publication of *The Fatal Conceit: The Errors of Socialism*.
1989	The Berlin Wall falls, revealing the abject failure of the central planning that Hayek had spent a lifetime criticising.
1991	Hayek is awarded the US Presidential Medal of Freedom.
1992	Hayek dies in Freiburg – now in a reunified Germany – and is buried on the outskirts of his native Vienna.

HAYEK AND
HIS INFLUENCE

"In the 1980s, Hayekian sentiments were translated into policy by Ronald Reagan in the United States and Margaret Thatcher in Britain. Markets were opened up to competition, Keynesian policy was abandoned, the State started to divest itself of loss-making public industries, efforts . . . were made to trim welfare budgets. The worldwide character of this reversal only became fully apparent with the collapse of Communism between 1989 and 1991. Hayek lived to see it all. In old age, he became the dominant intellectual influence of the last quarter of the twentieth century."

– **Keynes' biographer Lord (Robert) Skidelsky,** *Times Literary Supplement*, **1996**

Hayek's place in the history of ideas

FOR MOST OF the half-century following the second world war – and for much of that time, almost alone – Hayek kept alive the flame of personal and economic freedom in a world that had come to put its trust in planning and controls.

He argued that socialism, even democratic socialism and moderate state intervention, was founded on a mistake; and he dedicated much of his later life to explaining what this mistake was.

On the basis of his deep knowledge of economics, politics, philosophy, psychology and information science, Hayek concluded that socialist planners could never in fact assemble the vast amount of information they would need to run an economic system, because that knowledge – which market systems process easily and routinely every day – is dispersed, diffuse, incomplete and essentially personal, existing only in the minds and experience of millions of different people.

The socialist dream, therefore, would always be frustrated by reality; and as the socialists tried to impose more and more control on that reality, ordinary people would increasingly find their freedoms being stripped away.

More than anyone, Hayek gave intellectual foundation to these ideas, and showed how the free economy and the free society, though unplanned, are nevertheless highly organised – the evolutionary products of our constant adaptation to each others' values and actions. They contain a 'wisdom' that socialist planners cannot even understand, far less manipulate. Competition and the price system, for example, steer resources to where they are most valued, and do so far more quickly and effortlessly than could any planner.

It was principally for his early work on business cycles that Hayek was awarded the 1974 Nobel Prize in Economic Sciences. But his wider thinking on the mechanisms and merits of the market economy inspired a whole subsequent generation of economists, including many who would go on to win Nobel Prizes of their own – such as Milton Friedman, George Stigler, Maurice Allais, James Buchanan, Vernon Smith, Gary Becker and Ronald Coase. A 2009 study by David Skarbek showed that only Kenneth Arrow was cited more often in the work of other Nobel economists – an indicator of Hayek's influence on his profession.

Hayek gained admirers in other fields too. "I think I have learned more from you than from any other living thinker," the philosopher Karl (later Sir Karl) Popper wrote to Hayek in 1944; and leading neuroscientists have commented on the originality of Hayek's ideas on the nature of human perception.

Hayek's thinking also enthused a whole generation of intellectuals, writers and think-tankers, who in turn disseminated his ideas even more widely. Among them were Henry Hazlitt, journalist and co-founder of the Foundation for Economic Education; Ralph (later Lord) Harris and Arthur Seldon, who ran the Institute of Economic Affairs; F. A. ('Baldy') Harper who established the Institute for Humane Studies, Eamonn Butler and Madsen Pirie who set up the Adam Smith Institute; and many others around the globe.

Spread widely in this way, Hayek's ideas came to have a practical political effect too – something unimaginable for much of the half-century following the second world war. Politicians such as Margaret Thatcher and Ronald Reagan owed much to his thinking. So did the revolutionaries who became the political leaders of Eastern Europe following the collapse of Soviet communism: they read and translated his books in underground editions that would help change the climate of opinion. "No person," concluded Milton Friedman, "had more of an influence on the intellectuals behind the Iron Curtain than Friedrich Hayek." The fall of that Iron Curtain was indeed due in large part to him.

Today, all over the world, Hayek's ideas remain a guide and inspiration. Think tanks promote his views; student groups name themselves after him; college programmes spring up in his name; journalists cite him; academics admit their intellectual debt to him; and his views are analysed in books, papers and blogs. Millions of ordinary people owe to him their enjoyment of the fruits of economic and personal freedom, even though they may not know it. But then, as Hayek pointed out, knowledge is not always obvious.

The making of an economist

Friedrich August von Hayek was born in 1899 in Vienna, then the capital of the Austro-Hungarian Empire. His was a diversely academic family: his father was a doctor; one grandfather was a leading zoologist, the other a professor of constitutional law and president of Austria's Statistical Commission; the philosopher Ludwig Wittgenstein was a cousin; his brothers would become science professors.

Hayek initially showed an interest in science, too, but events would shift his interest elsewhere. With the first world war raging, he joined the Austro-Hungarian artillery on the Italian front, and served as a spotter in the ramshackle aircraft of the time, an experience he was lucky to survive. Human history was changing before his eyes: Russia was seized by communism, the Habsburg Empire collapsed. And in 1919, postwar Austria abolished the minor aristocratic 'von' titles, from which time he became just plain F. A. Hayek.

As the war ended, Hayek decided he must study economic and social issues rather than the natural sciences. He entered the University of Vienna, where philosophy and law featured in his studies. He earned a doctorate in law while still only 20, and two years later earned another, in political economy.

But Hayek did not give up his keen interest in science. In 1920, he worked briefly at the laboratory of brain anatomist Constantin Monakow, an experience that stimulated his insights on perception and the workings of the human mind – insights that would be crucial to his later thinking on economics.

At Vienna, Hayek – a voracious reader – came across the work of the 'Austrian School' economists, who emphasised the importance of individuals' values – and their freedom to act on them – for economic progress. One such was Ludwig von Mises. As well as being a private tutor at the university, Mises was running an office set up to resolve debt issues stemming from the Austro-Hungarian break-up, and was seeking young economists to help. Hayek had looked in on one of Mises's lectures, but had found it far too hostile to his own mildly Fabian socialist views: Mises had already published a paper arguing that socialism could not possibly work. But Hayek took the job, joined in Mises's seminars, and gradually found his own views changing – though not completely – as their collaboration deepened.

Inflation too was a powerful educator. Prices in Austria escalated wildly in the 1920s. In the space of just eight months, Hayek's salary was raised 200-fold, just to keep pace with prices that doubled each day; and the disruption that this hyperinflation wrought on society was clear to him. For the whole of his life, Hayek would regard inflation as a major, and avoidable, evil.

Such concerns led Mises and Hayek to set up a think tank on business cycles, with Hayek as its first director. Their research showed that bad government policy was the ultimate cause of these cycles. When the authorities made credit cheap by keeping interest rates low, or printed more money to finance their expenditures, it created a frenzy of borrowing and spending, a boom that must inevitably end in a bust. The analysis was powerful: Hayek predicted just such a bust for the United States, shortly before the 1929 Wall Street Crash and the Great Depression that followed.

This research, encapsulated in Hayek's books *Monetary Theory and the Trade Cycle* (1929), *Prices and Production* (1931) and later *The Pure Theory of Capital* (1941), brought Hayek fame as a macroeconomist. And he had a flair for promoting his ideas more widely: his letter to the *New York Times* on Germany's finances in the 1920s was only the first of his large output of 'letters to the editor' in the newspapers of many countries.

In 1928, Hayek's institute organised a London conference on economics. Leading British economists attended, including Sir William (later Lord) Beveridge, who would go on to design the postwar welfare state, and John Maynard (also later Lord) Keynes, whose economic thinking would dominate the postwar years.

Though Hayek and Keynes went on to become personal friends, they disagreed fundamentally on economics. After a spell as a tutor at Vienna, Hayek moved to the London School of Economics in 1931 to teach economics and statistics – and perhaps to balance the School's famously Fabian outlook – at the invitation of its head of economics Lionel (later Lord) Robbins. Within a year, Hayek and Keynes were exchanging pointed letters in *The Times*: Keynes advocated government spending to kick-start the failing economies of the time; Hayek believed that this policy would produce only indebtedness, inflation and disruption.

Yet in terms of their impact on policy debate, the methodical Hayek, an outsider with a broad Austrian accent that he never lost, was no match for the well-connected, urbane and intellectually agile Keynes. For example, Hayek spent a great deal of time writing a critical review of Keynes's *Treatise on Money*, fearing its inflationary consequences – only for Keynes to tell him that in the meantime, he had changed his mind on the issue completely. When, in 1936, Keynes published his *General Theory of Employment, Interest and Money*, Hayek did not bother to review it, believing that Keynes would probably change his mind yet again. But the book, which Hayek thought a mere "tract for the times" – the depression era – became a runaway success and set the tone for decades of postwar government intervention, expansion, borrowing and inflation.

The radical liberal

The second world war changed Hayek's life as much as the first. He sold many of his books on monetary policy and turned to political science instead. With the London School of Economics evacuated because of the blitz, Keynes found Hayek rooms adjoining his own Cambridge college, King's, where Hayek, frustrated at the hostilities, began a short book, *The Road to Serfdom*. He aimed to show how the moderate state planning that so attracted British intellectuals had morphed, in Germany, into totalitarianism – as it would elsewhere.

The book came out in 1944 and, hugely controversial, quickly sold out its initial print run. It impressed Britain's wartime leader Winston Churchill, and became an issue in the 1945 general election. It was also read by the young Margaret Thatcher, who later said she found it "the most powerful critique of socialist planning and the socialist state". It made Hayek's name in America, too, where tens of thousands of copies were sold, and *Reader's Digest* distributed another 600,000 copies of its own condensed version. On the back of this fame, Hayek lectured across the United States and became a visiting professor at Stanford University.

Shortly before the publication of *The Road to Serfdom*, Hayek's place as a leading British economist – he had been naturalised in 1938 after Hitler's Germany annexed his native Austria – was sealed by his election to the prestigious British Academy. The timing was lucky: another economist friend, Sir John Clapham, told Hayek that if the book had come out first, Britain's establishment academics would never have accepted him.

Hayek had also been exploring other ways to promote the critique of socialism and the case for a free society. At a meeting in King's College in 1943, he suggested forming an academy of classical-liberal scholars who might keep alive the ideals of economic and individual freedom, even though the intellectual tide had turned so much against them. In 1947, he did so – assembling 39 British, European and American thinkers for a ten-day conference in the Swiss resort of Mont Pelerin. Among those attending were Ludwig von Mises, Karl Popper, the historian C. V. (later Dame Veronica) Wedgwood, the young (and later, Nobel) economists Milton Friedman, George Stigler and Maurice Allais, plus Henry Hazlitt, F. A. Harper and Lionel Robbins.

The Mont Pelerin Society, as it became known, remained small for many years. This was, after all, a time when liberals like Hayek were very much in the minority. Communism had now gripped the whole of Eastern Europe; even in the West, the talk was of 'winning the peace' through the same sort of central controls that had been used to fight the war. State planning was seen as more rational, modern and efficient than a 'chaotic' market economy.

But thanks to Hayek, other seeds of liberty were being planted too. In 1946 a former RAF fighter pilot, Antony (later Sir Antony) Fisher, who had read *The Road to Serfdom*, sought out Hayek at the London School of Economics to ask how he could help promote its liberal principles. Hayek warned him off entering politics, arguing that ideas have a far more profound importance on events than any politician. Fisher took the advice, and ten years later set up the Institute of Economic Affairs (IEA), appointing Ralph (later Lord) Harris and Arthur Seldon to run it. Through the following decades, the IEA would challenge the intellectual assumptions of the day, issuing a barrage of reports and papers that showed the merits of free markets over state intervention in many different areas of public policy.

Hayek had also been deepening his understanding of the limits to social and economic planning. With *Collectivist Economic Planning*, in 1935, he brought the continental debate over socialist calculation – in which Mises was a principal contender – to the English-speaking world. A year later, he was writing on the crucial role of information in the economic system – dispersed and personal information that central planners could not possibly collect. In the early 1940s, he produced other papers showing how the human sciences such as economics were different in character from the natural sciences such as physics, making 'scientific' attempts to predict and control society fundamentally misguided. In 1946 he took this even further with his book on human perception, *The Sensory Order*, which argued that what we call 'facts' are actually the products of our own mental filing system – another warning to those who think that the 'facts' of economic life are simply out there, waiting to be collected and used by some benevolent planner.

The wilderness years

In 1950 Hayek took up residence in America, where his ideas had slightly wider resonance than in Britain. At the Committee on Social Thought in the University of Chicago, he taught social and moral science and conducted seminars on the philosophy of science that were attended by Milton Friedman and other prominent thinkers. He began working on the letters of the nineteenth-century libertarian philosopher (and author of *Utilitarianism*) John Stuart Mill, and started thinking about the history of liberal ideas and tracing their roots in authors such as John Locke, David Hume, Adam Smith, Alexis de Tocqueville and Mill. This would form the foundation for his next great book, *The Constitution of Liberty* (1960), a positive alternative to the dire warnings of *The Road to Serfdom*, finished in the Alpine tranquility of his native Austria.

But the book was out of tune with its times, even in America. The postwar economic boom now persuaded not just intellectuals, but politicians and the public too, of the merits of Keynesian-style government intervention and spending. Through the two decades from the mid-1950s to the mid-1970s, as what became known as the 'Keynesian Orthodoxy' picked up momentum, Hayek found himself scorned and isolated. These were his wilderness years.

In poor health and nearing retirement, he returned home to German-speaking Europe, taking up a post at the University of Freiburg in West Germany. There, he worked on his trilogy *Law, Legislation and Liberty*, in which he would explain the difference between the 'laws' and institutions that had grown up naturally through history and experience, and the 'legislation' laid down by politicians who mistakenly thought they could do a better job.

By then, what Hayek saw as the dire consequences of the Keynesian Orthodoxy were all around him. Inflation was reaching alarming levels, particularly in Britain. So Hayek returned briefly to pure economics, and to the boom and bust analysis where he had started with Mises. In *A Tiger By the Tail* (1972), he explained how inflation sabotaged the delicate workings of an economy and led to enormous waste. Inflation, he explained, stemmed from too much spending and borrowing by governments. Like a drug, only greater and greater doses of inflation could keep the Keynesian boom fantasy alive; but that must inevitably end in even greater disaster.

Changing fortunes

Hayek's wilderness years ended abruptly in 1974, when he was awarded the Nobel Prize in Economic Sciences for his "pioneering work in the theory of money and economic fluctuations" (his early work on business cycles) and his "penetrating analysis of the interdependence of economic, social and institutional phenomena" (his later work on the evolutionary nature of society). Hayek gave his Nobel Lecture on 'The Pretence of Knowledge', chiding economists and political scientists on their folly in trying to manipulate and steer social forces that they could not even understand.

The unexpected award gave Hayek a new lease on life – later he would say, "I tried old age but decided I didn't like it" – and gave his ideas and his support an international boost. He travelled widely, lecturing and being feted by universities. The Mont Pelerin Society he had founded grew fast, holding regular conferences around the globe. New policy think tanks such as the Fraser Institute in Canada and the Adam Smith Institute in London arose and promoted his views.

The new mood swept up practical politicians too. Margaret Thatcher, who had just been elected leader of the Conservative Party, met Hayek for the first time in London in 1975. Just months later, at a meeting of her party's HQ in which an aide was arguing the virtues of the 'Third Way' – a compromise between capitalism and socialism – she produced from her briefcase a copy of Hayek's *The Constitution of Liberty* which she banged down on the table, saying sternly "*This* is what we believe!" She later described Hayek as "one of the three great intellects of the twentieth century". Ronald Reagan too would list Hayek as one of the main sources of his individualist political philosophy.

Hayek was later awarded some of the highest honours that Britain and America could bestow. In 1984, Queen Elizabeth II made him a Companion of Honour (he described it as "the happiest day of my life"), and in 1991 he was awarded the Presidential Medal of Freedom by George H. W. Bush.

Vindication and legacy

The final volume of *Law, Legislation and Liberty* was published in 1979. This time, Hayek's work was embraced with enthusiasm – and not just in the West. His ideas were seeping through the chinks in the Iron Curtain, and bootleg translations of his books were starting to excite the intellectuals of Eastern Europe. Then in 1989, the Iron Curtain at last fell, exposing the grim reality of what Hayek had predicted of state socialism. New, younger, liberal revolutionaries replaced the Soviet old guard – personalities such as Mart Laar, the first post-Soviet prime minister of Estonia, and Vaclav Klaus, the prime minister and later president of the Czech Republic. Each discovered Hayek's ideas and went on to become prominent members of the Mont Pelerin Society.

Most Western intellectuals believed that what problems there might be with Soviet communism could be put down to individual personalities and cultures, rather than any fundamental fault in the idea. Only Hayek and his liberal colleagues had maintained that the whole edifice was built on a mistake and that it would largely extinguish human freedom, before inevitably collapsing. He lived just long enough to see his predictions borne out by events, and the intellectual tide turn at last in his favour. He died in 1992 in Freiburg – by then in a reunified Germany – and was buried on the outskirts of his native Vienna.

He left many legacies. There was his prodigious output of books and articles. The Mont Pelerin Society, which continued to expand as a focus and forum for free-market thinkers and activists around the world. The think tanks set up by his followers. Academic centres such as that at George Mason University, for whom his thought provides both a foundation and a guide for new thinking on the free society and free economy. Ultimately, though, his legacy is the continuing debate provoked by his ideas – appropriate for one who always maintained that it is ideas, not politicians, that have the real power to make the world a better place.

UNDERSTANDING
SOCIETY

THE DESIRE TO RECONSTRUCT society is a common one. We all see laws and institutions that we disapprove of: the urge to sweep them away and replace them with new ones is strong. We constantly re-shape the physical world to make it serve our purposes better. Why should we not re-shape society? After all, we humans made these laws and institutions. Surely we can change them?

We can indeed, said Hayek, but we cannot be sure that the result will please us. Society is a highly complex arrangement, and it is not obvious how the changes we might want to make will affect its overall workings. Often, our well-intentioned reforms produce quite disastrous consequences. That is because we are dealing with something that is indeed human, but which we do not – and indeed cannot – fully understand.

That, believed Hayek, is because our social institutions are the results of our own human action, right enough – but not the product of our deliberate design.

Order without planning

This can be a difficult idea to get to grips with, because we tend to divide the world into 'natural' and 'artificial' (or 'invented') things. The first set we imagine as wild and unstructured; the second we see as deliberate and orderly. Since social institutions have an orderly structure to them, we presume that they have been deliberately invented – which in turn suggests they can be re-invented. But both presumptions, said Hayek, are wrong.

There is, he insisted, a third category of things: those which have an orderly appearance, but which have *not* been consciously designed by anyone. The regular V-formation of migrating geese, for example, or the order we see in a hive of bees, does not exist because one particular goose or some particular bees have ordained it. These things are orderly, but natural. The same occurs in human societies. Language, for example, is very orderly, with regular grammatical rules. But nobody ever designed the world's languages: they grew up naturally as we strived to communicate. The market economy, likewise, is a very orderly system of human exchange, said Hayek. But it did not just pop into some inventor's head: the market, and market institutions such as money and prices, gradually emerged and evolved over many centuries as people bartered and traded with each other.

The idea that useful and smoothly functioning systems can grow up without being deliberately intended and designed by human beings – what Hayek called *spontaneous order* – has a long history. In *The Constitution of Liberty*, Hayek traced it back to writers such as John Locke and the eighteenth-century Scottish thinkers Adam Ferguson and Adam Smith. Of course, they did not have the theory of evolution to explain things, and could only attribute this happy state of affairs to providence or a deity. Today, by contrast, we recognise that orderly systems, even very complex ones, can evolve naturally: and not just physical ones like our own bodies, said Hayek, but social systems too.

Orders are built on rules

The problem for those who want to change society is that it is very hard to know how the behaviour of individuals contributes to the overall social pattern. For example, observed Hayek, worker bees engage in constructing cells, cleaning cells, and foraging at different times of their lives. Yet it seems very unlikely that any worker bee realises that she is acting in any regular way, or acts in that way with the specific purpose of helping create the overall social order of the hive. And even intelligent observers like us would have difficulty predicting precisely how any change in that behaviour – workers doing more foraging and less cleaning, say – would affect the overall pattern of life of the hive.

The overall social order, then, depends on there being some regularity in how individuals behave – what Hayek called the *rules* of individual conduct – but not necessarily in an obvious way.

Certainly, it may be obvious that no society would last long if its members had no qualms about killing each other on sight or stealing each other's property. That is why successful societies have evolved with moral or religious codes prohibiting murder and theft – and more. (Indeed, many of the regularities in individual conduct that make human society viable are of this negative sort – that we *do not do* certain things – rather than the sort of positive calls to *do* certain things that the social engineers commonly urge on us.) But take another case where the link between individual action and the overall order is not so plain. As people walk from one village to another, noted Hayek, they save themselves effort by walking on the ground trodden flat by earlier walkers. In the process, they wear away a hard path that makes the walking easier for everyone. It is not their *intention* to create a path. Nor is it public-spiritedness, because they have only their own convenience in mind. Yet their actions create an outcome that is good for everyone.

According to Hayek, the market economy is another example of a beneficial overall order that, paradoxically, rests on self-interested behaviour. People buy and sell goods solely for their own benefit: they want what other people are willing to sell, and other people want what they are willing to sell. Yet from this simple, self-interested behaviour has grown up the price mechanism and a worldwide trading order that (as we will see) efficiently steers goods and services to where they deliver most value to producers and consumers. Selfish private action can produce a beneficial public result.

It is easy to see why radicals who want to re-make society might be confused. The truth is that we have but scant understanding of how the regularities of individual conduct – the rules of morality, religion, law, habit and custom – build up into a beneficial social order. Human society, though ultimately the result of human actions, is really much too complex for any human mind to comprehend. Yet without that understanding, believed Hayek, we cannot be sure how even the slightest change in the rules will affect the overall result. It might upset the balance of this delicate system and lead to chaos: we can never be quite sure. But the attempts of social engineers to replace our hugely complex social order entirely with some construction of their own will almost certainly prove to be a catastrophic mistake.

> "[B]efore we can try to remould society intelligently, we must understand its functioning; we must realize that, even when we believe that we understand it, we may be mistaken. What we must learn to understand is that human civilization has a life of its own, that all our efforts to improve things must operate within a working whole which we cannot entirely control, and the operation of whose forces we can hope merely to facilitate and assist so far as we can understand them."
>
> – F. A. Hayek, *The Constitution of Liberty*

Rules contain knowledge

Hayek was not an inflexible conservative, though. Our moral and legal rules do change, he observed, and indeed it is essential that we do adapt our practices to changing circumstances. That is how society evolves. Yet our best guide to what might work in the future remains what has worked in the past. The rules of action that we follow – often without even thinking about it – have at least brought us this far. They contain, he said, a certain wisdom or *knowledge* that serves us well. The zealots who seek to tear down the social order and substitute instead their own blueprint – *constructivists*, Hayek called them – overlook this *knowledge content* of established social rules, putting themselves at a serious disadvantage for their task.

The knowledge content of our rules of action is not limited to the knowledge of particular objective *facts* – knowledge *that* something is the case. Perhaps more importantly, they contain knowledge of *how to act*.

This is the sort of knowledge we gain when we acquire skills, for example. A skill is not a set of 'facts' that we can write down and pass on to others; it is a form of personal – in the jargon, *subjective* – knowledge of what to do in certain circumstances, which we each have to learn for ourselves. Likewise, said Hayek, our habits, customs and even our emotions and gestures are all vital to making social life work, but that does not require us to understand or explain their importance in the overall social order. Rather, we simply follow them, often without thinking about it, and they play their part in helping us get along.

Hayek saw this as an evolutionary process. Groups in which the various rules of individual action mesh together to produce a beneficial overall order will prosper, expand, and replace others. So these rule systems gradually become more prevalent, whether or not the individuals concerned understand the relevance of their actions to that overall success.

Three kinds of rules

Hayek identified three sorts of these behavioural regularities. The first is those rules that are deliberately chosen – the principles and laws set out by constructivists who have their own blueprint for how they think society should be built.

The second is the rules that we follow, even though we may be unable to describe them in words – the rules of 'fair play', for example, or our 'sense of justice'. These rules can be very much more complex than those set out in the reformers' blueprints: it is doubtful, said Hayek, that anyone could set out all the things encapsulated in the idea of fair play or of justice. Yet, rather like the complex rules of grammar that we learn through experience, we do not need to be able to describe, or even understand, these rules in order to learn and use them.

The third group is the rules that we follow on the basis of learning or nature, but which we also try to set down in words. Common law is an example of this. On the basis of judgements upon individual cases over the centuries, we try to identify and write down a number of legal principles. But these remain only an attempt to approximate in words some specific elements of the idea of justice, said Hayek – an idea that is actually very complex and hard to express.

The existence of the second and third sorts of social rules means that people who think they can reconstruct society by imposing new and consciously chosen rules may well find themselves thwarted by other behavioural regularities that prove even stronger, despite the fact that they may not be expressed, understood or even noticed. And they will struggle to establish how these various rules of conduct interact with one another to produce a working social order – depending as it does on millions of individuals constantly adjusting their behaviour to one another, on the basis of innumerable, unfathomably complex rules of personal action.

The benefits of rule systems

In a very small group where the individuals all know each other, it is relatively easy for them to predict how their actions will affect other people, and will affect the group as a whole. But that is clearly impossible in the vast, extended societies of today. We can know only a tiny handful of the thousands that make up a town, or of the millions that make up a country; it would be simply impossible to know how our individual actions would affect every one of them, how they would react to what we did, and what impact that would have on the society as a whole. That is why modern human societies, said Hayek, depend on individuals following *rules of conduct* – on people behaving in certain regular and predictable ways. This behavioural regularity allows us to cooperate with others easily, and even without even having to think about it. It is like a skill – the skill of knowing how to act.

Not only can rule-guided societies be larger, said Hayek, they can also be far more complex. A society that is directed by some central authority is inevitably constrained by the amount and complexity of information that this authority can collect and process. Its very ability to survive changing events is limited by the authority's ability to understand and control what is going on.

In rule-guided societies, by contrast, the knowledge of how to act in different circumstances is spread across many millions of individuals. Those individuals will have a more direct understanding of their local circumstances than could any distant planning authority. It all means that rule-guided societies are able to adjust to changing events far more quickly and effectively than centralised societies.

So while it is certainly possible to construct social arrangements based on principles that we consciously choose, those societies will inevitably be much smaller and far more limited in scope than our vast rule-driven societies of today. We cannot simply reconstruct modern society as we choose, concluded Hayek – at least, not without facing the threat of it collapsing into chaos.

Growth not reconstruction

Yet the fact is that societies do change. Indeed, the evolution of a social system based on individuals acting in certain regular ways *depends* on that behaviour adapting to changing circumstances. But such evolution is gradual, the result of many small changes rather than a few wholesale reconstructions.

As events unfold, explained Hayek, we constantly evaluate whether our rules of conduct are still appropriate to the new times, and modify them accordingly. That might well throw rules into conflict with each other – as we see all the time in the conflict between the attitudes of different generations, and in court disputes about which legal rules should apply in particular cases. Ultimately we may need to abandon some rules and values that we feel are less important than others. It is a process of constant re-evaluation and change.

But it is re-evaluation and change within our existing fabric of rules and values. We are not clever enough to soar above our civilisation and produce a better one by tearing up and re-weaving that fabric. How could we soar above it, asked Hayek, when our own minds have evolved as a part of that civilisation? When conflicts arise, the only yardstick we have is consistency: how well a rule fits in with all the others that we adhere to, for the most part unthinkingly.

Evolution of modern society

Hayek likened the evolution of rule-guided social systems to the evolution of the sense of sight. Just as sight allowed animals to respond to events at a distance, the development of rule-guided systems allowed individuals to coordinate their actions with the behaviour of millions of others whom they do not know.

He speculated that human society started in small hunter-gatherer groups. Each would be regulated by its own ethics and customs. Members would follow these rules, not because they understood their significance to the group, but because evolution pushed them to – groups which adhered to beneficial rule systems would prosper, and those that did not would fail.

We cannot know all the various changes in social rules that allowed us to expand from such early groups and made possible the vast, extended human society of today – what Hayek called the *extended order* or the *Great Society*. But it must have involved various rules being modified or abandoned at various times, and new rules being adopted. Hayek suggested that early hunter-gatherer groups would probably practise a simple form of socialism. It was probably accepted that some person in authority would assign the tasks of daily life between the group's members; there may well have been a presumption that food should be shared. But one can imagine how bartering with other communities gradually created the idea of private property and the laws that protect it – an economy built on property, trade, self-interest and contract, rather than on the ethics of sharing or of central direction.

Our ancestors probably never suspected that their bartering would lead to the development of money, prices, property rights, contract law, specialised trades and the other features of the modern global economy, said Hayek. Many group members might even have been shocked at this affront to authority and their culture of sharing. Yet it was only the fact that we abandoned the simple socialism of the old culture, and adopted new rules and values, that made the emergence and growth of the Great Society possible. Instead of the inevitable limits placed on our development by a system that works only where people know each other closely enough to share tasks and resources, the move to rule-guided systems allowed us to coordinate our activities with millions of unknown people all over the world, to the benefit of us all.

We did not adopt this elaborate new network of rules because we were clever enough to see its universal benefits. It simply evolved because it worked. Those who could restrain their hunter-gatherer morality could form larger societies and grow in number, and the new rules kept spreading.

Even so, the old morality, which served us for the hundreds of thousands of years that we spent in small groups, remains deeply embedded in our instincts. When the new rules conflict with the old, we still yearn for the simple socialism of the past. But our lives and prosperity depend entirely on our having muted those yearnings. As Hayek put it, we have been civilised against our wishes.

Essentials of the new morality

Hayek suggested that three very important sets of rules formed the spine of this new morality and the civilisation we have built upon it – the rules of private property, honesty and the family. We did not necessarily understand the great benefits of these new rules, but just by adopting them, we gained an edge that helped us expand our numbers.

It is easy to see how the rules of private property would benefit groups. It allowed trade between different individuals and communities, such that each could exchange things they valued less for things they valued more. That in turn allowed people to specialise in producing particular goods and services for exchange; they could then develop their skills and tools and so make their production more efficient. And this greater productivity generated greater wealth, on which the population could grow.

Individuals might have seen benefit for themselves in property and trade, but many of the new rules would take the form of restrictions on what the individual could do. Often, they would be bound up in systems of religious belief, giving them even more power and authority – which, contended Hayek, is why religion has played an important role in human progress. The only religions that survive long, he observed, are those that uphold the new morality of property, honesty and the family. (Communism, he suggested wryly, was a modern religion, but its relegation of the family and rejection of private property meant it could not last.)

A self-regulating order

Some people may be alarmed at the population explosion unleashed by this new morality. But Hayek believed the phenomenon to be self-limiting.

He saw economic advance and population growth as greatest at what he called the 'periphery' of development, where the old values meet the new. In the older form of society, people use their wealth to create larger families, which improves the prospect of survival for themselves and for their group. People in the rich countries of the new morality no longer use their wealth to create larger families because the new rule system itself ensures their survival and comfort.

The teeming shanty towns around many rapidly growing cities provide an example, said Hayek. Those who live in them are not an underclass pushed out by capitalism; rather, they are people who are able to raise children by living off a little of the expanding wealth of those nearby cities. Without capitalism, those people would not be alive at all. But as capitalism expands and their prospects improve, their children and descendants have less need for the insurance policy of large families.

So the most rapid growth, in prosperity and population, occurs at the interface of the old and the new values – where old and new cultures come into contact, or in societies where the old values are giving way to the new. But as the institutions of the market economy embrace more and more of the world, observed Hayek, this interface must shrink, and the population explosion will be over. We will apply our wealth to other purposes. And falling birth rates in developed economies back up Hayek's point.

Is Hayek right?

To sum up, Hayek argued that society is not something we can simply rebuild the way we want it. It is a complicated order that builds up from the regular actions of individual members, but not in an obvious way. It is not something that we have deliberately designed – or could deliberately design – because its workings are beyond our comprehension. It has simply evolved and spread because it works. We may pine for an earlier morality that served us well when we lived in small groups, but this is just a throwback – an *atavism*, as Hayek called it. Our very survival depends on us having changed from this old, face-to-face kind of sharing society to one built instead on general rules of action that allow us to collaborate with millions of other people whom we do not even know.

Some critics are troubled by this idea that evolution selects between entire systems of group morality, seeing it at odds with the rest of Hayek's writings – where he emphasises the importance of the individual, and argues that we can only explain social phenomena, such as markets, in terms of the motives and behaviour of the individuals involved.

But Hayek is perfectly consistent. It is true that in recent years, there has been an active debate about the level at which the selection of physical characteristics occurs, with most biologists placing it at the level of *genes* or clusters of genes. These vary greatly between individuals, but not greatly between different human populations, meaning that there is little for group selection to work on. Some people conclude that ideas, customs and values – what the evolutionary theorist Richard Dawkins calls *memes*, being the cultural equivalent of genes – must also be selected at the individual level. However, social and cultural characteristics *do* vary greatly between populations, making selection at group level perfectly plausible. Yet as economist Douglas Glen Whitman points out, memes only get to this group stage of selection once *individuals* have chosen to adopt them. Individuals are a *part of the selection process*; memes are filtered both at individual and at group level, and there is no contradiction in Hayek's views.

Another criticism is that Hayek has far too much faith that this process of cultural evolution will produce an optimal result. After all, says British economist Andrew Dennis, it has also produced institutions that are harmful to most of us, like the Mafia. Nor, says political scientist Norman Barry, does it even produce the things which Hayek himself values: state regulation prevails over free markets in most societies. Hayek's over-optimism, say these critics, make him too traditionalist, defending the status quo against serious change. A different system might work better: we cannot know until we try it.

In fairness, Hayek actually rejected the idea that evolution produces *optimal* results. Things do not have to be perfect to survive, just good enough: or if there is competition for resources, just a little better than others. Nor did he claim that traditions are necessarily 'good' or that our institutions are always moral. He said only that since we do not understand the relevance of our traditional behaviour in terms of the overall order, making big changes carries a big risk. The best we can do is review our rule systems for consistency and, where they conflict, drop the rules that we *believe* are less important.

Other critics say that individuals would only act in ways that (unknown to them) promote the overall social order if the action benefitted them personally. What then is the incentive? And in any event, the conduct of any one individual must have a vanishingly small impact on the vast societies we have today. So can Hayek's mechanism really work?

Yes, it can. Individuals do not necessarily have to see benefit for themselves in doing what ultimately benefits the group as a whole. Religious and moral codes, for example, require people to curb their own desires. They may feel that such restraints harm their immediate personal interests; but they accept them in the hope of attaining an afterlife, or of avoiding the disapproval of others. Those religious and social pressures have evolved precisely because they help to restrain individual behaviour, and so provide the group with an edge.

It is not the action of any single individual that provides this edge – that would indeed be a tall order. Rather, it is the actions of millions of individuals, all acting in regular ways and avoiding particular types of behaviour that would ultimately damage the whole group, even if the individuals do not know it.

FREEDOM AND
THE LAW

Why freedom is crucial

HAYEK BELIEVED that individual freedom is crucial to the evolution of complex societies. By *individual freedom* or *liberty*, Hayek had in mind the state in which *coercion* is minimised. That is, where people are not generally forced to act according to the will of someone else, under the threat that some even greater evil will be imposed upon them.

Many writers of course see personal freedom as good in itself, and therefore as something to be promoted for its own sake. Hayek agreed, but argued that it also had a critical role in social evolution. In his view, individual liberty is a basic *precondition* for a flourishing and dynamic social order and the benefits that go with it. It is not a good that can be traded off against other things; it is absolutely essential to the health and growth of our society. He gave two reasons for this.

First, as we have seen, Hayek maintained that our economic and social system is far too complex for anyone fully to understand. We simply do not know how changing our personal behaviour will affect the overall order. As it is, the rules that we voluntarily accept contain a measure of 'wisdom' that helps produce a successful overall outcome. If instead someone else forces us to act in other ways, the likelihood is that the result will be worse. And the greater the number of people that are coerced into acting according to someone else's will, the greater is the probability of disaster.

Second, freedom allows us to capture the opportunities thrown up by what is unpredictable. If we are all allowed the freedom to experiment, then some of us may stumble across better ways of doing things. We can all then build on that discovery and seek out the next improvement. That is the way human societies make progress – how new ideas are developed, new tools fashioned, and new threats overcome.

But progress is not something you can command – nobody knows where the next useful discovery will come from. We cannot plan for what cannot be foreseen. All we can do is to create the conditions that make it more likely that people will come up with new and beneficial discoveries. And that means maximising their scope to experiment and explore new ways of doing things. It means maximising their freedom.

There are vast possibilities for human progress if we allow people to try their own ideas. No authority is better at coming up with new ideas than an entire population of free people. A free civilisation is hugely creative. But if we do not leave people free to innovate and solve problems, warned Hayek in *Studies in Philosophy, Politics and Economics*, "we must not be surprised if society, as such, ceases to function as a creative force."

Freedom allows people to make their own guesses about how best to act, and to take their own risks in the limited context of their own lives and circumstances – rather than having to trust the whole of humanity to the single guess of some authority. Some people argue that society nowadays is so complex that it cannot be left to itself and must be planned. Hayek believed the exact opposite: a free society is so creative and so complex that it could never be managed by the conscious mind of any planner.

Freedom is for everyone

It is true that we can never know in advance whether the specific actions that free individuals take will ultimately prove beneficial or harmful to the social order. But we do not support freedom because of what it produces in specific cases, argued Hayek. Rather, we support it because in the long run, it produces more benefit than it does harm. Freedom would not work if it was restricted only to actions that we knew in advance would prove beneficial. Its creative power would be stifled, and people would never discover those novel and unforeseen improvements that their freedom to experiment throws up.

"Our faith in freedom does not rest on the foreseeable results in particular circumstances but on the belief that it will, on balance, release more forces for the good than for the bad."

– F. A. Hayek, *The Constitution of Liberty*

Nor should we restrict freedom to what the majority feel comfortable with. The fact that only one person in a million wants the freedom to do some particular thing is no reason for preventing it – because that oddball's freedom might just throw up some novel improvement that benefits us all. If we are to enjoy the creative benefits of freedom, freedom must be as general as possible.

Freedom and the state

To Hayek, liberty meant minimising coercion. Sadly, coercion cannot be avoided altogether, because the only way to prevent people coercing others is to threaten force against those who try it. Who, then, should wield this ultimate coercive threat – and how do we ensure that this coercion, too, is kept to a minimum?

Free societies, said Hayek, solve this problem by confining the use of coercion to the state, rather than any individual. For the most part, the coercive force of the state is used to *prevent* people breaking the behavioural rules, rather than to *make* them act in particular ways: only those who break the accepted rules of conduct are subject to state coercion. So individual acts of coercion such as robbery, blackmail and violence are discouraged by the threat of punishment by the state.

However, we may occasionally want to make people do more than just *avoid* harmful actions, observed Hayek. Sometimes we want to make them *do* certain things for the general benefit – like paying taxes or fighting in the army during times of war. But this immediately raises the question of where the limits to such state coercion should lie. Plainly, we should not allow the state to force us to do *anything* which those in authority deem fit. That would certainly not be a free society; and no human beings, with all their imperfections, could be trusted to wield such enormous coercive power.

So to prevent the immense coercive power of the state from being abused, said Hayek, we need to restrict its use to enforcing a strictly limited list of duties that we all accept and understand. Setting limits on how the state's monopoly of force can be used at least spares us from arbitrary or growing coercion by other people who happen to be in authority.

"Liberalism for this reason restricts deliberate control of the overall order of society to the enforcement of such general rules as are necessary for the formation of a spontaneous order, the details of which we cannot foresee."

– F. A. Hayek, *Rules and Order*

In other words, a free society is not one without rules or government power, but one in which government itself is limited by predictable rules – the situation Hayek called *the rule of law*.

Laws versus justice

One of the reasons governments commonly go beyond their proper limits, believed Hayek, is people's confusion about the nature of the law. We call any measure that is passed by a government assembly a 'law' – but this disguises important differences between two very different types of measures.

Probably the bulk of measures passed by governments, he believed, are simply *administrative orders*, designed to run the machinery of government and tell public servants how to operate. In a collectivist economy, of course, all measures are of this kind, since the government manages everything and everyone is a public servant. It is a system built on the *commands* of authority.

A free society, by contrast, is built on a framework of *rules of conduct* – regular ways of acting that are commonly accepted and observed. They may be enshrined in moral or religious codes, or in a deep public sense of justice. That does not mean we can always describe exactly what they are. We simply take them as a 'given' because they evolved as part of our mentality, and we follow them almost without thinking, precisely because they benefit the whole population. These rules are not something that the government authorities can successfully change at will.

One role of the authorities, however, is to try to define more accurately what these commonly accepted rules should be. Occasionally, disputes arise as to whether or not a rule is being broken, and cases are brought to court. What the court has to do is to decide which side is right, and why. This process, said Hayek, requires the legal authorities to try to put into words what the rules really are. Sometimes the rules have not even been articulated before; or sometimes a previous court has tried to explain them, but still left room for dispute. The task remains the same: to attempt to crystallise our intuitive ideas of justice into language as accurately as possible – and to do so against the background of the existing fabric of rules. The legal process is not about *creating* new laws, but about *discovering* what the existing rules of justice actually are.

The rule of law

It is because people confuse the two kinds of lawmaking – issuing new administrative commands and putting the established rules of justice into words – that it is so crucial to set limits on government actions. Governments can issue whatever administrative commands they want; but we cannot allow them to believe that they can re-state the rules of justice as they deem fit. That would be a very dangerous delusion.

Hayek's notion of the *rule of law* does not tell us what particular laws there should be. It simply gives us some principles by which we can judge laws and proposed laws, and check that they do not violate the rules of justice.

First, he contended, people must retain some *private sphere* into which the law does not intrude: our private conduct is no business of legislators. Second, laws should not discriminate in favour of or against any particular person or group: laws should *apply equally* to everyone, even to those who have not yet been born. Third, laws must be *known and certain* – or at least must express the rules of justice as accurately and consistently as we can. That in turn means that laws should *not be retrospective* – because nobody could know how to behave in order to avoid falling foul of some future retrospective law.

Socialism and the law

Under the rule of law, everyone is bound by rules, even the government itself. Though we may have long-established legal traditions such as *habeas corpus* and the right to trial by jury, said Hayek, it is unlikely that our liberty could survive without a basic acceptance and belief in some general rules that bind everyone, including the authorities.

Under the rule of law, government and private action is judged against the background of generally accepted rules, not on the basis of what social outcome some official wishes to promote. The role of a lawmaker or a judge is to uphold and clarify those rules that have worked well. If officials and judges ignored the rules and simply chose whatever outcome they preferred, warned Hayek, respect for government and the legal process would quickly break down.

Socialist measures therefore do not pass the test of the rule of law, said Hayek. They are designed to produce a particular outcome, such as the achievement of an overall economic plan. They intrude into the private sphere because they regard individuals as subservient to the plan. They do not treat people equally because they assign them particular roles in pursuit of that plan. They cannot be known and certain, because the roles of individuals must be continually re-assigned in order to meet the demands of changing circumstances. Socialist measures replace *rules* by *commands*.

Under the rule of law, by contrast, the authorities do not seek to determine what overall social outcome we should aim to produce, or who should do what, or who should be the winners and the losers. They aim simply to clarify and fix the rules that have served us well so far, and that have produced a generally beneficial social outcome, even though we have little or no understanding of how they do it.

Questions about coercion

Again, critics have taken issue with Hayek's views on freedom and the rule of law. Ronald Hamowy, for example, argued in a 1961 article ('Hayek's concept of freedom: a critique') that Hayek's idea of freedom as the absence of coercion could lead to some strange results. Plainly, if someone invites you to a party, but insists you wear formal dress, you are being put under pressure by the host, though nobody, Hayek included, would call this 'coercion'. But if your non-appearance at this party threatens one of the things you most value, your social prestige, would most people not then regard the dress code as 'coercive'?

Or to take another example: people voluntarily buy and sell water all the time. But if I own the only oasis in a desert, a traveller's only alternative to buying it from me is to die of thirst. Most people would regard that as a coercive relationship. So at what price does the relationship cease to become voluntary and instead become coercive?

Hayek accepted none of this. Coercion, he said, is where the pressure to conform to another person's will puts people in a worse position than they would otherwise have been. The host's demand to wear formal dress is not coercion because the invitation, even with that condition, extends the possibilities that are open to the guest. The guest's prestige anxieties do not alter that.

But the water in the desert question is different, said Hayek. In normal markets, it does not matter how much the seller charges: if the buyer is willing to pay that price, the transaction is voluntary on both sides, and therefore not coercive. Nor does it matter how essential the service is to the buyer – the buyer is still in a better position after this voluntary exchange than before it. But if someone has a monopoly supply of something so essential as water in the desert, the reality is that we expect different rules to prevail. We would wish the seller to recognise a moral obligation to supply water to people who would die of thirst without it. We count on such essentials, and justly regard monopolists' refusal to supply them on normal terms as immoral.

Questions about the rule of law

Hayek's concept of the rule of law also troubles some critics. Libertarians, for example, have lamented that he specifically allowed conscription within his concept of the rule of law, even though forcing people to risk their lives seems to be the greatest possible intrusion into the 'private sphere'.

Hayek responded that freedom does not mean eliminating coercion, but minimising it. We cannot eliminate coercion entirely. As long as some people are prepared to attempt to coerce others, as long as robbery, fraud and violence abound, we will need coercion to discourage them. The same applies in the case of conscription, said Hayek: some countries – such as Switzerland – regard the evil of conscription as fully justified in order to protect the community from the greater evil of coercion by outside forces.

Hayek insisted that our aim should be to limit the coercive power of the state to where it is unavoidable as the only way to discourage coercion by others. We do not want anyone to be able to pretend that this coercive power can or should be used in any other circumstances. Hence, the use of that power must be subject to general, abstract rules – rules that are known and apply equally to everyone, including the government authorities themselves.

Hayek accepted that this rule of law principle, that laws must apply equally and not single out particular groups, could still allow widespread restrictions on freedom – such as America's 1920–33 Prohibition law. But that, he thinks, is as good as it gets. If legislators were *really* bound by the same laws as the rest of us, and could not find ways round them, it is probable that even measures like Prohibition would have a hard time getting through the legislature.

THE MARKET
PROCESS

THE DESIRE OF some people to redesign society is never stronger than in the field of economics. Again, their assumption is that anything that is not consciously designed and planned must somehow be wild and unkempt. They talk about the 'chaos' in markets that fluctuate daily, the 'duplication' of competition and the 'waste' that is advertising. Economic production and distribution, they conclude, could be made far more 'rational'.

Such attempts to redesign the economy on more 'rational' grounds were never more widespread than in the times in which Hayek lived and wrote. Much of Eastern Europe became gripped by communism, and the idea of total state control of the economy spread to China and Southeast Asia, gaining traction in South America and Africa too.

The battle lines today are different. After the fall of the Berlin Wall and the practical experience of decades of communism, people are more inclined to recognise the productive power of markets than they once were. The debate is more about how those markets should be restrained and regulated. But while Hayek's writings focused on the shortcomings of comprehensive state planning, his arguments remain relevant to the modern debate. His view was that those who want to impose their own vision on economic life simply misunderstand how markets work – that like other social institutions they are a living, growing product of an evolutionary process. Consequently, any interventions, no matter how wholesale or piecemeal, are bound to produce unexpected – and almost certainly unwelcome – results.

Divergent values

What Hayek called the *market order* – the overall pattern of free economic activity – is not chaotic but structured and orderly. It is another example of an evolved, rule-guided social order. In markets, people buy and sell, and provide goods and services to one another, according to established rules of property and contract – rules which, again, come so naturally to us that we hardly have to think about them.

Therein lies the enormous advantage of the market order over the social engineers' attempts to impose some particular economic vision. In markets, people with very different ideas and objectives can come together and trade things for mutual advantage; they do not have to agree on anything beyond that. But where people's actions have to conform to some overall objective, then either everyone has to agree on that aim, or be forced to comply. The first is unlikely; the second is coercion.

Getting people to agree on things is never easy. But the market system works precisely *because* human beings disagree about things, said Hayek, and it builds advantage on that very disagreement. *Value* is not some scientific quality of objects, like their weight or size; it is something in the *mind* of each individual. Different people value the same things differently: someone who buys a good plainly values that good more than the money they have to pay for it; while the seller values the money they get more than the good they give up.

To illustrate this point that the market process makes use of our differences, Hayek invited his readers to consider a simple bartering process, such as may have happened between different human groups long ago. If each had an excess of something the other wanted, then both sides would benefit from exchanging their surplus with the other. They would each get something they valued *more* in exchange for giving up something they valued *less*. Even if they were enemies, both would still benefit from the trade. Indeed, and perhaps astonishingly, the more they disagreed on things, the easier it would be for them to trade. The *greater the difference* in the value they each put on a particular good, the *more benefit* they would each gain from exchanging it.

All they needed to agree on, in fact, was the rules by which they traded things.

Economic interdependence

Today this simple system has evolved into a vast marketplace that covers the whole world; and we are no longer limited to bartering with the people we meet. Through the medium of money, and following the broadly understood and widely accepted rules of property and exchange, we can now trade indirectly with unknown millions of other people in other countries. Countless producers trade with countless manufacturers, who trade with shippers, who trade with wholesalers, who trade with retailers, who trade with customers. Each of those transactions benefits both sides: as the pioneering economist Adam Smith pointed out in 1776, they would not accept the bargain if they did not each benefit. The result is that we all get what we want, what we value, thanks to a little of the industry of a great number of others.

This is the great strength of the market order, Hayek believed. It allows the whole population of the world to cooperate voluntarily, even though they do not share common aims and values. It is hard to imagine any other system that could reconcile the world's differences so harmoniously. Certainly, it would be difficult to get any large group of people, or group of countries, to agree on a common economic vision, which is what socialist planning would require. It is odd but true that the unity of mankind depends upon our economic relations and our pursuit of private satisfaction.

So if there is a role for economic policy in economic life, as Hayek believed, it is not to try to impose some specific order on it, but to let the rule-guided market order flourish – to clear away barriers and increase the ability of all the unknown millions in the world marketplace to pursue and achieve their own diverse purposes. It is that freedom that makes the market order so creative.

The market telecommunications system

The market economy, then, is not like an army, for which objectives are set and where individuals are assigned the specific tasks needed to achieve those objectives. It is more like a game, said Hayek – an interactive, wealth-creating 'game' where players follow the rules and benefit from being in the game, but where the final outcome – what will be produced, and how, and what the various 'players' will end up with – is uncertain. Indeed, nobody would willingly play the game if the result was known or decided in advance, since it is the very prospect of changing the outcome that spurs people into the wealth-creating risks and effort that ultimately benefits all the players.

The market system is, moreover, an interactive game, in which each player has to take account of the moves of all the other players. To succeed, producers have to respond to the demands of customers; customers have to scan the market for good value and low prices; and people competing for the same resources have to reach some kind of agreement. An interactive game like this obviously requires some way for all the players to communicate with one another; but how can we possibly communicate with the unknown millions of other participants in this worldwide game of wealth creation? The answer, said Hayek, is breathtakingly simple. We connect with every one of them through the telecommunications system of prices.

In the market order, the rewards to each participant depend on the prices at which they can sell their goods or services in the market. But those prices will reflect the value that others set on those products. The more strongly that people want the seller's product, the more they will be willing to give up in exchange to get it. That is, the more they will pay – or in other words, the higher the price. Prices, therefore, act as *signals*, said Hayek, publicly indicating to everyone where their product is most highly valued, and prompting them to steer their efforts and expertise in those directions.

"The manufacturer does not produce shoes because he knows that Jones needs them. He produces because he knows that dozens of traders will buy certain numbers at various prices because they (or rather the retailer they serve) know that thousands of Joneses, whom the manufacturer does not know, want to buy them."

– F. A. Hayek, *The Mirage of Social Justice*

And amazingly, prices encapsulate all the information that producers and customers need. Suppose that some new use for tin is suddenly discovered, or that a major source of tin becomes exhausted, suggested Hayek. With tin now more scarce, its price will rise. But traders do not actually need to know the reason – all they need to know is that the price of tin has risen, so they must economise on it. They must use less, or turn to some substitute for tin. The extra demand for the substitute will in turn bid up its price, and prompt those using the substitute to seek yet other materials to substitute for that; and so it goes on. The entire market order adjusts to the shortage of tin, even though hardly anyone knows what caused it.

This certainly gives markets the edge on any form of central economic direction or planning. Economic planners would need to know what possible uses there were for tin, why people wanted it, and what substitutes were available, before they could even start to work out how to deal with its new scarcity. But the market adjusts automatically, explained Hayek, processing all that information into a simple signal – price – that is the only thing people need to know. Like an engineer keeping a machine in adjustment simply by watching one or two gauges, the participants in the market order adjust to each other's actions simply by watching prices.

"In abbreviated form, by a kind of symbol, only the most essential information is passed on and passed on only to those concerned. It is more than a metaphor to describe the price system as a kind of machinery for registering change, or a system of telecommunications which enables individual producers to watch merely the movement of a few pointers, as an engineer might watch the hands of a few dials, in order to adjust their activities to changes of which they may never know more than is reflected in the price movement."

– F. A. Hayek, *Individualism and Economic Order*

Information and the market

Hayek believed that the price system is able to communicate much more subtle kinds of information than most people imagine, or than planners could collect. There is a tendency, he warned, to think of human knowledge as a single whole, a unitary body of information that is accessible to everyone. But it is not.

Today, a trawl on the web would bear out Hayek's point. There is a vast amount of information out there, but it is not always easy to find what you need. Much of what is set down as true is in fact only the opinion of particular experts or groups, and is contradicted somewhere else by others. Or it is simply mistaken; or maybe just a part of the truth, with other parts lost in some different corner of cyberspace. Nor does the information get to people equally fast: some people have only slow access, or none. Even those with fast access could never scan the whole of human knowledge that exists online, or keep up with the daily additions to it, or resolve its conflicts and fill in its gaps. Yet the information that is written down on web pages is only a tiny fraction of the knowledge that exists in the minds of the world's billions.

Much of this dispersed knowledge changes rapidly. Hayek took the example of the knowledge possessed by real estate agents, who have to spot fleeting opportunities in a rapidly shifting market, matching the needs of particular buyers to the properties available; the knowledge of the shipper who profits by chartering otherwise empty cargo vessels on their return journeys; and the knowledge of the foreign currency dealer who gains from the momentary fluctuations in exchange rates. This is all local, changing, unorganised knowledge that would be no good to a central planning agency – indeed, it would be out of date even before it arrived there.

And there is the special, personal, *subjective* knowledge that people have about their own values, needs and changing circumstances. Sometimes we do not even realise what value we attach to different things until we are faced with a stark choice. We may struggle to express our values in words, never mind communicate them. Then there is the expert knowledge of the entrepreneur who correctly anticipates what customers want. And the skill of the producer who, like an artist, knows just how to mix different inputs to create something that people will value. These are all kinds of deeply individual information which cannot be shared at all, but which the market collects, processes, transmits and uses.

In Hayek's view, then, the greater part of the information that the market process deals with automatically is dispersed, partial, personal, local and fleeting – precisely the sort of information that it is impossible to collect and process centrally. That is why our best efforts at economic planning have proved so inept.

How markets maximise benefits

Through the price system, the market process conserves the things we value – such as our time, our effort, and our materials. The buyers of tarpaulins, suggested Hayek, probably do not care whether they are made from a base of hemp, flax, jute, cotton or nylon. Tarpaulin producers therefore choose the material that provides a serviceable product at least cost – that is, with least sacrifice of materials that have other, more valuable, potential uses elsewhere.

In this respect, the price system is something of a 'marvel', claimed Hayek. It is blind and issues no orders, yet it steers resources to their highest-value uses and squeezes out waste and inefficiency. But we did not invent this mechanism: we simply stumbled upon it, since it emerged naturally out of the process of our trading goods and seeking out the best value.

The market is not based on people obeying orders, or working hard, but on people creating and delivering products and services that other people value, and doing so in ways that conflict least with others. Market rewards reflect the value that we deliver to others – and provide the incentive to keep us delivering it. We can never be sure of the exact outcome of this rule-guided game of wealth creation, but it creates opportunities, and provides benefit, to everyone who participates in it.

The process of competition

Our lucky discovery of the price mechanism allowed our economic system to expand hugely, because it made use of widely dispersed, personal knowledge and enabled the diverse purposes and actions of millions of different people to be coordinated peacefully. But for the price mechanism to work at its best, *competition* is essential. Competition among producers – and consumers – is what drives the bargaining that determines what prices will prevail. It is a vital part of the market system – not something that wastes resources or duplicates effort.

You would not realise this from the textbook description of 'perfect competition', complained Hayek. This abstract idea supposes that all producers (and all consumers) are alike, trade products that are identical and share the same (perfect) knowledge of their market. So duplication is built in to the model. The trouble is not so much that such uniformity could never happen, but that this picture utterly distorts what competition actually is.

Plainly, knowledge is never perfect. No producer knows for sure how much of a product customers will buy, and at what price: customers may not even know that themselves, until the choice is put before them. Nor are any two producers – doctors, say, or grocers – exactly alike. Consumers too are all individuals with different needs, outlooks and values. Products are not homogeneous – indeed, competition pushes suppliers to *differentiate* their products and to try to convince customers that theirs are better, or cheaper, than others. It is this that drives product innovation and progress.

Competition as a discovery process

Hayek therefore regarded competition not as a settled state of affairs, but as a dynamic activity, a *discovery procedure* in which producers are constantly searching for new ways to satisfy customers, and consumers are constantly on the lookout for products they prefer. Because producers' technologies and consumers' horizons are always changing, markets are in constant flux.

It is competition that prompts producers to experiment with new and different products in the hope of satisfying demands that others have missed – and to do so quickly, before a competitor fills the gap. This is the role of the *entrepreneur*, to seek out and fulfill previously undiscovered opportunities for satisfying the public's wants; and it is competition that stimulates such innovation.

The role of profit in this should not be dismissed or forgotten. Hayek believed it obvious that the market rewards that come from successfully satisfying other people's wants provide a powerful incentive for people to try. Profit is not some kind of undeserved windfall, but the reward for serving the needs of others – and an inducement to do so. Successfully serving others is something we *learn* to do through the process of acting competitively. By contrast, an enterprise such as a government monopoly, which has no inducement to seek out new opportunities, never learns how to serve consumers better, and never adds to human progress.

Knowledge must be discovered

The textbook perfect competition model suggests that we can identify the point where the producers' supply of goods and consumers' demand for them comes into balance. Indeed it suggests that we can do the same for every product, and build up a neat picture of what products should be produced at what prices in order to bring the whole economic system into perfect balance or 'general equilibrium'. This thought heartens those who would like to see the economy planned 'scientifically' or 'rationally', for it suggests that with a bit of calculation we can identify exactly what range of products should be produced and in exactly what quantities.

Hayek rejects this as a *fatal conceit*. Knowledge, such as the knowledge of what might satisfy market demand, is personal – *subjective*. People have to discover it, and different people may discover different things or interpret what they discover in different ways. And since events change constantly, the answer will change too – something that is particularly important in an economic system where changes in one market, like that for tin, produce knock-on effects in every other.

Nor do we know how the millions of people involved in the modern market order will respond to changes. Each has their own system of values, but those values may be very different. Often, as already mentioned, people do not know exactly what they will plump for until they are confronted with the choice. How individuals will react to changes in events is of course crucial information in terms of its economic effect and consequences; but this is information that is deeply private and widely dispersed. It could not be collected by a planning authority, even in principle.

So it is an illusion to think that we can simply collect the facts and describe an entire economic order in terms of a few mathematical equations – or any number of them, for that matter. And the idea that we can then direct our efforts to produce this supposedly optimal collection of goods is a decidedly dangerous illusion.

If there is any identifiable balance in the market order, said Hayek, it is what might be called *dynamic equilibrium*. In any market, supply and demand will tend towards balancing each other, but the constant changes in people's reactions to events and to the actions of others means that markets will never actually settle. Like a stream flowing downhill, he said, things flow in a general direction, but currents and eddies form all the time. Only when we understand that the market order can never be static, that people's reactions to constant change can never be predicted, and that markets are a dynamic *process* will we begin to understand the futility of trying to command economic events.

MONEY, INFLATION,
BOOMS AND BUSTS

T HE MARKET ORDER, then, is a very extensive and sensitive arrangement. Prices and production depend on complex interrelationships between people, and between people and things. Change is constant, and small changes in one part of a market have effects that spread out everywhere, like ripples in a pond. As the whole system adjusts, it is quite possible that minor changes at one point can have profound consequences at many others.

Hayek lived through turbulent economic times. He experienced at first hand the hyperinflation in his native Austria and in Weimar Germany, where money lost its value so quickly that banknotes became a cheaper fuel than wood. Then there was the Wall Street Crash of 1929 and the Great Depression that followed; the New Deal era of massive government expansion; the postwar redesign of the international monetary system; the inflation and the stagflation – rising prices but faltering output at the same time – of the 1960s and 1970s.

Hayek's own work on these issues serves to illustrate the key role of the price system, and how the delicate mechanism of the market can be disrupted – and the whole market order thrown into chaos – by the policy mistakes of the authorities.

Boom and bust cycles

Since the beginning of the nineteenth century, economists have sought to explain the seemingly regular up and down fluctuations in economic activity – the *business cycle* or *trade cycle*. So it was that, in 1927, Hayek and Mises founded the Austrian Institute for Business Cycle Research, with Hayek as its first director, in their own attempt to understand the nature and causes of these fluctuations. It was this research that would allow Hayek to predict the inevitable crash that, in 1929, rudely ended the 'roaring twenties' boom in America.

Hayek and Mises saw these boom–bust cycles as rooted in problems with money and credit. Mises had already written on this subject, and another leading Austrian School economist, Eugen von Böhm-Bawerk, had earlier pointed out the importance of credit availability and interest rates for the pattern of business investment. Over a decade from 1927, Hayek successfully integrated all these strands of thought in a series of important books and articles on money, capital, credit and what is now known as the 'Austrian Theory' of trade cycles. It was a remarkable achievement for an economist still in his thirties.

According to Mises and Hayek, the business cycle is really a *credit* cycle, because it starts with an increase in the amount of money that banks lend to their customers. That in turn is usually the result of policy decisions made by central banks. Central bankers, and their political masters, like booms. When things are going well, they get praised; during slowdowns they get only criticism. So naturally they want business to boom. The way they engineer that is to cut interest rates.

Central banks are such large players in the financial markets that by lowering the rate at which they lend to other people – mainly the commercial banks – they drive down interest rates right across the financial sector. Since the banks can now borrow more cheaply, they can also afford to lend more cheaply. They cut loan rates for their customers, who can then afford to borrow more. So families take out new or bigger home loans, and entrepreneurs take out business loans to build new factories and equipment. Suddenly, there is plenty of money about: people are spending freely, and everything appears to be on the up.

But in fact, said Hayek, the artificially low interest rates set by the authorities disturb the delicate market mechanism of prices – since interest rates are the price of borrowing. This 'false signal' of cheap credit sets in train a series of unintended consequences that will eventually turn the boom into a painful bust – with bankruptcies, closures and unemployment.

How banks magnify money

The central banks' artificial lowering of the price of borrowing is mischief enough, but its effects are magnified by the way that banks work, the so-called *fractional reserve* system.

It is strange but true that, by taking their customers' cash and lending it out over and over again, the banking system actually creates money. If you deposit £100 in your bank, it does not stay locked in the bank's vaults, waiting for you to withdraw it again. Instead, the bank plays the odds and keeps on hand only enough to meet the day-to-day withdrawals that customers do make – which might well be as low as 5% of their total deposits. So the bank can lend the remaining £95 to other customers. They of course use that money to buy things from suppliers, who deposit it in their own bank – which in turn keeps 5% (just under £5) on hand for day-to-day withdrawals, and lends just over £95 to other customers, who then buy things from suppliers who deposit the money in their bank . . . and so the cycle continues. Your original £100 deposit has been magnified into deposits totalling many times that.

The importance of this, according to Austrian School thinking, is that a small rise in bank credit, contrived by the central bank, can snowball into a big economic problem. Lower interest rates encourage customers to borrow, creating deposits that the banks recycle over and over into further loans. Soon, the banks have created a huge amount of money, all balancing on a very small foundation.

The boost to business

To borrowers, though, it looks like enormously good news. Loans are cheap and plentiful, people have more money to spend, and businesses can afford to expand their production to capture that extra spending. Businesses dash to invest, equipping themselves to supply new or more sophisticated products.

Indeed, said Hayek (building on the ideas of Böhm-Bawerk), the credit boom will entice producers into more 'roundabout' or 'longer' production processes. With finance now cheaper, producers can afford to take longer over production before bringing their goods to market, perhaps adding details or refinements or new features that customers too can now afford more easily.

In other words, the new cheap borrowing causes a change in the structure of production, and in the type, scale and location of the capital goods (such as buildings and equipment) that are used to create it – what economists call a 'deepening of the capital structure'. Though the cause may be artificial, its economic effects are decidedly real and physical.

Boom turns to bust

Up to this point, the boom looks set to stay. But as more entrepreneurs see profit to be made and join the dash to invest, the increased demand for land, buildings and equipment starts to push up the prices of these capital goods. At the same time, producers' increased demand for labour starts to bid up wages too. Businesses start to find things getting tight.

By now, though, entrepreneurs are deeply committed to their new investments. They have built the factories, bought the new equipment, and hired the workers they need to take advantage of the apparent boom. Their costs are rising, but if they pull out now, they will have nothing to show for their investment. Like a builder who has oversized some foundations and then run out of bricks, they try to keep borrowing in the hope that they can yet finish and save their projects.

Sadly, observed Hayek, the new money that the banks have created is starting to run out. They have lent as much as they can. Nor are the banks pulling in so much money from savers, who see no point in saving so much at the new low rates of interest. Running short of cash, the banks start to worry about the security of their loans – tightening their terms, raising their charges and even demanding repayment from the customers they regard as most risky.

Now we are in a credit crunch. With prices rising and loans harder to get, projects that seemed profitable when credit was cheap begin to look over-optimistic. Businesses start to fail under the weight of unsustainable commitments; workers are laid off; investment and spending fall; and commerce goes into decline. Some firms will default on their loans, causing the banks to tighten their terms even more, which will squeeze other firms into bankruptcy too. Even firms that acted prudently, said Hayek, will find themselves caught in the tidal wave of cutbacks and failures.

From fake boom to real losses

However, the banks' return to more prudent lending does not *cause* the crisis. It simply exposes the overambitious, mistaken investments that occurred because credit was artificially cheap. But those, said Hayek, are exactly the sort of mistakes that people make when prices are distorted – in this case, the price of credit. People have responded to the *false signal* of artificially low interest rates by borrowing too much and making mistaken and non-viable investments – what he called *malinvestments* – on the back of it.

Despite the tide of failures, there may still be profit in shorter, less sophisticated and less costly production processes, like those that prevailed before the boom phase of the cycle. But by now the whole market order has become dislocated: resources are in the wrong place, and are of the wrong kind, to serve the changed realities of customers' demand.

It is true that some buildings, equipment and tools might be re-used for other purposes; but a great deal of sophisticated capital equipment is designed for only one specific purpose. A high-volume newspaper press, or the sophisticated equipment in a car plant, for example, is not much good for anything else once the newspaper or the carmaker has gone bust. These investments simply have to be written off. Likewise, workers in defunct enterprises might be re-trained for other jobs; but the only available jobs may be in a different part of the country, and the necessary re-training will cost time and money.

It all means that real resources are wasted. The fake boom induced people to waste time, money and effort on production projects that could not actually be sustained. The boom produced only an inevitable bust, with a real loss of capital and real unemployment.

Blame the authorities

If you blame anyone for this, it should be the central banks for starting everyone on the boom–bust cycle in the first place. They were trying to boost business, but their artificial manipulation of interest rates caused knock-on effects to other prices as well, and spread a disruption through the whole fabric of the market order. The boom they created was not the start of new prosperity but the start of an economic disaster.

Unfortunately, there is no way out, except to let interest rates and prices adjust back to reality. The boom was like a drug that delivered a high; the bust was the inevitable hangover. Just like a drug, people get habituated to boom times. Only larger and larger doses of credit can keep the high going and hold off the hangover for a little longer. But that spiral cannot last forever, and just makes the hangover, when it comes, even worse.

So in *Monetary Theory and the Trade Cycle*, Hayek was explicit in placing the blame for the length and severity of the Great Depression on the 'forced credit expansion' policies of the Federal Reserve back in the 1920s – and then their continuation of cheap credit policies through the 1930s, which they hoped would help business to pick up after the crash. In fact this 'hair of the dog' cure simply prolonged the agony by continuing to lull people into poor investment decisions, rather than letting the market correct the massive mistakes that had already been made.

Indeed, the Federal Reserve's policy throughout this episode was more damaging still. As the monetary economist Milton Friedman subsequently showed, the Fed precipitated the 1929 Crash, and made it more severe, by causing the amount of money in circulation to fall. That was like throwing a speeding car into reverse, rather than just touching the brake to slow it down. Incomes that had been rising on an inflation spiral now fell sharply as banks and businesses ran out of cash – causing huge disruption everywhere.

Hayek certainly believed that there was no other cure for the boom–bust cycle than to go through the downswing of write-offs, factory closures, business failures, layoffs, falling wages and a slump: the mistaken investments have to be abandoned, so that whatever capital might be rescued can be invested more usefully elsewhere. But for Hayek, a downward spiral of deflation, with tumbling incomes and prices, was just as damaging as an upward spiral of inflation. Both are rooted in the unreality of incompetent central bank policy, and both disrupt the delicate mechanism of the price system. The aim of policy should be to set the financial conditions by which the nation's income grows at a sustainable rate, and to avoid such damaging swings in money and credit.

Hayek versus Keynes

Nothing caused more disagreement between Hayek and John Maynard Keynes than this point. Keynes did not see a slump as the inevitable consequence of an earlier boom; he put it down to problems with the capitalist system itself. His solution was to boost 'demand' – the willingness and ability of people to buy things – including 'investment demand' for capital goods, something he thought was essential to generate new production and employment.

But in Hayek's view this expansionary policy leads only to greater disaster. The problem is not a *shortage* of investment, but *malinvestment* – investment that has gone to the wrong places. It is not a *shortage* of demand, but a *mismatch* between demand and supply. Artificially low interest rates have prompted business to commit real resources to unsustainable projects that are designed to produce things that people no longer want or can afford.

Keynes therefore makes a crucial mistake in wanting to boost 'demand' or 'investment'. He is looking only at the *totals* of what people buy or invest, not *what* they want to buy and *where* and *how* they are investing. If the things that producers are geared up to supplying are different from the things that customers are demanding, then no boost to *total* demand, however large, will correct the mismatch. By lumping different things together, Keynes has obscured the real problem and therefore comes up with the wrong solution.

But what Hayek called the "final disaster" is Keynes' belief that only governments could engineer the new demand that was needed to end the slump. Not only is this the wrong solution; it also encourages the belief that government policy is the source of high or low levels of business activity and employment. That, thought Hayek, credits government with an expertise it does not have. It was, after all, government efforts to boost business that created the unintended catastrophe of the boom–bust cycle. That is hardly a great record of economic management.

Keynesian measures, therefore, will only make a slump worse. Keeping interest rates low only encourages more of the over-borrowing that caused the market dislocation that started off the whole sorry cycle. Government efforts to boost 'investment' and 'demand' through public spending on projects such as roads, bridges and other infrastructure will hijack resources from where entrepreneurs might invest them more productively – and still not cure the mismatches in supply and demand that are the underlying problem.

The monetarist view

Milton Friedman agreed with Hayek on many things, but held that his 'credit cycle' explanation of boom and bust did not fit the facts. Changes in credit policy, he maintained, were simply not large enough to explain major episodes like the Great Depression. The cause, he thought, was not credit, but money.

He thought the blame belonged squarely in the same place – the central bank – but with its creation of money rather than its encouragement of borrowing. A central bank can simply print new banknotes and exchange them for IOUs from the government or the commercial banks – giving the government or the banks more money to spend, which then fuels a boom. These days there are other high-tech ways of achieving the same result. The key thing is that the injection of this new money into the economic system makes people feel richer, so they go out and spend – which prompts businesses to expand to capture that demand.

But as people rush out to spend the new money that the central bank has created, continued Friedman, prices are bid up and up. Before long, people find that they are really no better off at all be-cause the extra cash in their pockets is eaten up by the rising prices. This is the effect known as *inflation*. Again, if the central bank kept administering larger and larger injections of new money, it could keep the boom going – but that can only lead to acceler-ating inflation and to the ultimate chaos of *hyperinflation*. The sole cure is to curb the expansion of money and endure the resulting downturn.

To Friedman, it is the central bank's monetary expansion and the resultant bidding up of the price level that is the problem. Hayek agreed that it was the creation of new money that causes an artificial boom that can only end in a real bust, but he argued that commercial banks, through the magnifier of the fractional reserve system, create far more of it than do central banks. So it is cheap credit policies that remain the ultimate cause of the cycle.

But Hayek's main objection was that, rather like Keynes, Friedman obscured the real problem by lumping different things together – talking about across-the-board rises in 'the price level', for instance, instead of the *relative* movement of individual prices. Rather like honey pouring onto a table and forming a mound in the middle, insisted Hayek, new money (however it is created) will bid up prices at the point where it first enters the economic system. It will pull productive resources from existing uses and towards seemingly booming markets where prices and profits are high. And the same thing will happen at every point on the mound. The result is a widespread change in the pattern of production – but one made in response to false price signals, rather than in response to genuine demand. What makes the whole episode so damaging is that when the boom inevitably subsides, a large proportion of these mistaken investment changes have to be written off as the mound of inflated prices flattens again.

Inflation versus unemployment

In the late 1950s and beyond, some Keynesian economists argued that a mild rate of inflation could be tolerated, because its stimulating effect on business would boost employment. In other words, there would be a *trade-off* between inflation and unemployment. Hayek thought this completely wrong – contending that inflation of any amount would actually *generate* unemployment.

The reason, as the honey example illustrates, is because money is not 'neutral'. When new money is created, it does not instantly hit every corner of the economic system, bidding up all prices simultaneously. It is injected at some point, causing price rises to start there first and then ripple out through other markets. With different prices rising at different rates, entrepreneurs become confused by these false signals and cannot see clearly where to invest their money and effort to get the best return; inevitably, they make costly mistakes. Even a mild inflation will cause investment mistakes that will accumulate, one on another, for as long as the inflation lasts. That stifles the efficiency of markets, reduces competitiveness and leads to waste and unemployment.

We should be wary of any policy of inflation, said Hayek, however mild; for when the initial boost wears off, there will be calls for increasing doses of it just to keep the stimulus going. With each such rise, the mistakes multiply and markets become increasingly inefficient. If the authorities try to moderate the inflation rather than letting it accelerate, the result is *stagflation* – inflation and unemployment at the same time – something that Keynesians cannot satisfactorily explain.

With inflation rising, there may be calls to curb it through wage and price controls. But this, said Hayek, merely attacks the *symptom* of rising prices, not the cause – the excess of credit and the distortion of relative prices that it produces. The controlled prices, being artificially low, will encourage consumption but discourage production, leading to further mismatches; and artificially low wages will make employers take on more workers rather than invest in more efficient machinery, producing yet further misallocation of resources.

Inflation must be stopped dead

Since the only way out of the situation is pain now or even greater and more prolonged pain in the future, Hayek concluded that "inflation must be stopped dead". It is not an easy solution: the longer that inflation has persisted, the more mistakes will have accumulated. So the greater will be the economic mismatches, and the larger the scale of the inevitable closures and layoffs as these mistakes and mismatches are corrected by the new reality. There will be a surge in unemployment – but, Hayek believed, only for a comparatively short period. Stopping the inflation dead reassures people that it will not revive, so at least the foundations are laid for a real and lasting recovery.

Job losses will be higher in some industries than others – specifically, in those that benefited most from the inflation in the first place. People will have to relocate. That makes it essential to have a well-functioning labour market.

But we are unlikely to have well-functioning markets of any kind when people think that government has both the power and the duty to keep unemployment down. That belief will only drag government into the same sort of boom–bust policy mistakes all over again. The resulting inflation will lead to demands for government to be voted even more powers and controls. It is a vicious circle in which governments resort to greater and greater controls in the attempt to deal with problems they cannot possibly command. "Inflation," thought Hayek, "is probably the most important single factor in that vicious circle." If we want to stop the drift towards increasing government power, we should focus our attention on monetary policy.

Preventing inflation

Unfortunately, though, governments can create as much money as they want. They are no longer limited by the gold standard, which meant their notes and coins had to be redeemable for a fixed quantity of gold, and which therefore limited the amount of notes and coins that they could issue. As always, governments face the constant temptation to print money; today, they have the means to do it and not much to stop them.

> "With the exception only of the 200-year period of the gold standard [1714 to 1914 in Britain], practically all governments of history have used their exclusive power to issue money in order to defraud and plunder the people."
>
> – F. A. Hayek, *Choice in Currency*

Some people who worry about this lack of restraint on governments, and the policy disasters it can generate, believe in a return to the gold standard. But the economic and political hurdles are high. Hayek instead proposed another, startling solution, outlined in *Choice in Currency* and *Denationalisation of Money*: namely, end governments' monopoly on issuing currency and have it provided by the competitive market instead.

The idea may seem astonishing, since issuing money is so widely regarded as something that must be done exclusively by governments. But that has not always been so, and need not be so. If private issuers (such as banks) could produce their own different currencies, argued Hayek, people would naturally choose to use the most stable, least inflation-prone ones. The need for competing issuers to keep the value of their currency stable – or lose out to competitors who did – would give them a strong incentive not to issue too much.

That, believed Hayek, would go a long way towards sparing us from the boom–bust policy mistakes that have caused us so much distress over recent decades.

> "Government would be deprived not only of the main means of damaging the economy and subjecting individuals to restrictions of their freedom but also of one of the chief causes of its constant expansion."
>
> – F. A. Hayek, *The Political Order of a Free People*

PSYCHOLOGY,
SCIENCE AND
SORCERY

WHEN HAYEK was young, he did not know whether to become an economist or a psychologist. In the event, he went on to make important contributions in both fields – and in philosophy and social science too.

Hayek's thoughts on human psychology, first drafted when he was only 20, are an astonishing breakthrough in their own right; but they also powerfully support his economics. His analysis of how human beings observe and understand their world is highly relevant to his view that the 'facts' on which any economic system must work are fundamentally *subjective* – being the values, opinions and imperfect understandings that exist only in the minds of the millions of individuals concerned. Hayek explained that the way we understand things is filtered through our past experience – and that human reason, far from being able to soar above our world, is an essential part of it.

Hayek's observations on scientific method also explain why he thought social engineering a mistake. The social sciences, he insisted, are quite different from the physical sciences. They do not deal with inanimate and predictable objects, but with human beings, who have their own unpredictable motivations, purposes and values. While we may be able to detect broad patterns within human societies, we deceive ourselves if we think we can scientifically control them.

How we interpret our world

Traditional theories of human perception – how we become aware of our world – presume that there is a real, objective world outside us, which throws out information about itself that we somehow catch with our senses – sight, smell, hearing, touch and taste. Our minds then collect and sort this raw information – grouping similar sights or sounds, for example – and from this we can start to make sense of the world.

These theories are wrong, asserted Hayek in *The Sensory Order*. They make a false distinction between the human mind and a real world outside it. In fact, we too are part of the world and our minds are a part of us. Our minds do not stand apart from our environment and sense it from afar; our minds are a part of that environment. Our image of the world is not carried into our minds by sensory cells and nerve fibres – it is something created in our own minds.

To explain this, Hayek suggested that, over our own lives and over the evolution of our species, we come to learn that some stimuli – particular sights or sounds, say – tend to go together. On the basis of repeated associations, we *classify* things, in our minds, into different categories of events. We do not see the properties of an object, like red or loud, as unique to it, but see them as qualities that the object shares with others in the same mental filing-tray.

When any new experience comes along, the way we assess its relevance to us is to try to work out where it fits among the mental classifications that we have already built up. Perception, therefore, is not an act of receiving data from an ordered world: it is the act of us ordering our own mental image of the world – classifying and interpreting our sensory information against the filing system we have already built up on the basis of past connections.

Learning and progress

Sometimes, said Hayek, we are faced with new experiences that do not fit neatly into our pre-existing mental filing system. That forces us to adjust our categories and re-classify a number of our past experiences. This, in fact, is how we learn and make progress – constantly revising, improving and refining the way we understand the world. But it is our *minds* we are re-organising, not the real world.

Furthermore, we can only carry out such a revision within the overall structure of pre-existing mental categories that have been built into our minds through our evolution as a species and our past learning as individuals. We can only re-evaluate one part of the structure on the basis of the understanding we have derived from the other parts. That is how we see the world: we might learn to see some parts of the world in different ways, but we cannot tear up our whole understanding and see the entire thing differently. We simply would not have any reference point from which to start making sense of anything.

Mental and social orders

The organisation of our minds, then, is a mental or *sensory order* that has many similarities to our social and market orders. It is an orderly structure, but one that we have never consciously designed and do not fully understand – how could we, when our understanding is itself a part of it? Rather, it has simply evolved and grown because it brings us benefits. It enables us to interpret and respond to our environment by classifying things according to their abstract qualities – qualities that are important to our survival and prosperity (think of *sharp* or *poisonous*, for example).

And it gives us the mental framework from which we can revise and refine our view of the world, and learn to deal more effectively with our environment.

This is not so different from the market order – another orderly structure that we did not deliberately create, but simply stumbled upon. It too has evolved and spread because of the benefits it brings to those who are part of it. It too is a *discovery procedure* in which we learn how to respond to changing events. And like the sensory order, the 'facts' that the market organises and processes are in reality mental constructions – the personal, *subjective* interpretation of events that exists in the minds of those involved.

Our reason cannot replace such social orders, because it has grown up as part of them. The process has made us good at recognising linkages or patterns. We recognise 'justice' or 'fair play' when we see it, just as we recognise 'red' or 'loud', because our minds have evolved precisely to draw out such regularities as an aid to survival: but we may not be able to describe in words exactly what it is that defines any of these qualities. We can certainly learn – reviewing our rules and reclassifying things where there are conflicts: but we cannot somehow put our minds outside the whole system and redesign it. In other words, we are bounded by the inevitable limits of our reason. Our minds are part of that same system, and we can only see things as images or patterns – sensory, social or economic – that have been filtered through past experience, and judged against the existing fabric of ideas, customs and institutions.

The natural and social sciences

Such evolutionary limits on our reason should be a warning to social engineers. So too should Hayek's analysis of the differences between the natural and social sciences, which is found in *Scientism and the Study of Society* and subsequent writings. It is not surprising, he said, that social scientists want to emulate the obvious success of the natural sciences in explaining and improving things. But if they do not understand the differences, the results could be catastrophic.

Natural scientists, said Hayek, seek to find relationships between physical objects. Science can show us that ice and water are in fact the same thing. Once we have established these regular relationships, we can use them to help predict – and control – the behaviour of natural objects.

But the uncritical application of this extremely useful method to the social world is a grave error, which Hayek calls *scientism*. Natural scientists try to stand back from the natural world and explore its regularities without contaminating those findings with human judgements. But the social scientist's subject matter is human behaviour and human relationships. When we try to eliminate human judgements and values – the aims, motives, ambitions, beliefs, relationships or emotions that make them do what they do – we eliminate everything that is important to how society works.

We can certainly describe human behaviour in mechanical terms, said Hayek, but it is hardly informative. A carved stone dug up by an archaeologist is no more than that – until we ask what *reason* its creator had to carve it. As objects, a steam hammer and an ordinary hammer are quite different things – until we reflect on their *use* to human beings. Money is just paper and metal – the interesting thing is *why and how people choose to exchange it* for other things. No physical description could explain the prices of wool or iron, and *why* that causes people to demand more or less of them.

In summary, the subject matter of the social sciences is human beings and their values and intentions. Any attempt to explain the behaviour of human groups without bringing in people's motivations, insisted Hayek, is doomed to failure. But identifying and explaining people's motivations is far from easy.

Errors in social science

Hayek's view that natural and social sciences were entirely different changed somewhat from the 1940s onward, partly due to the work of his philosopher friend Karl Popper. Popper argued that all science is a process of prediction and testing. A theory is advanced, its predictions are then tested by experiment, and if those predictions do not stand up, it is rejected. Some other theory is then needed, and it is subjected to the same procedure. By this method, we winnow out bad theories and leave ourselves only with those explanations that, for the moment at least, seem to predict things well. This 'scientific method' is just as valid for the social sciences as it is for the natural sciences.

These insights caused Hayek to moderate his blanket criticism of social scientists trying to emulate the method of natural scientists, and to focus instead on some of the key mistakes to which they were prone. One such error is *behaviourism*, which describes human action in terms of its practical appearance alone. But as Hayek said, to understand human actions at all, we have to understand what *motivates* them.

False measurement is another common error, he believed. Precision is useful to the natural scientist, but you cannot assign numbers to human values, emotions or relationships.

A further mistake is *collectivism* – lumping different things together. Too often, thought Hayek, people talk of a 'country', or 'society', or 'capitalism' as if they were unitary wholes. But that conceals the wide diversity that exists between the relevant individuals, and all the complex relationships that really explain things – such as family, language, money, crime or punishments. *Statistics* too, though they have their uses, lump different people together and deliberately ignore the differences and the relationships of the individuals concerned.

Hayek also warned against *historicism*. This approach (exemplified in the works of Karl Marx), suggests that there are no general laws of social behaviour that apply in different societies or epochs, and that the only general laws are the historical laws of how one epoch (feudalism, say) turns into another (mercantilism). Both ideas are nonsense, said Hayek. There *are* some general laws, he insisted: even if the prices that applied in feudal England and ancient Egypt were obviously different, we can still be certain that monopolists in either would charge higher prices. And historical inevitability suggests that individuals have no control over their fate, but are somehow shaped by 'society'; when in fact the opposite is true: it is *individuals*, and the relationships between them, who comprise and shape 'society'.

The *false assumption of deliberate design* is another common mistake, said Hayek. Social scientists often ask what is the 'purpose' of a custom, tradition or some other social institution. What they really want to know is the *function* of these institutions in terms of the operation of the whole social order; but the use of the word 'purpose' suggests the existence of some conscious design. But as Hayek reminds us, the bulk of our social and economic institutions were not 'designed' by anyone.

The last error is *social engineering*. Like natural scientists, social scientists want to manipulate and improve things. This is folly, said Hayek. Mechanical engineers can know all the relevant facts about the physical objects they manipulate; but social engineers cannot possibly know all the relevant facts about the people they are trying to manipulate. Working out what capital goods were needed for optimal production, for example, would require a planner to know everything about the availability, location and uses of capital goods, and what value they would each produce for different consumers. That is an impossible task, not just because the amount of information required is so huge, but because it is so fragmentary and so personal – how can we know other people's values?

Making social science work

To be considered genuine sciences, then, the social sciences must come up with theories that predict things, and which can in principle be refuted by evidence. Hayek struggled hard to establish whether that was possible.

The tradition of the Austrian School was that social events are impossible to predict. Human beings are complicated creatures, and do not behave with the regularity of physical objects. We cannot easily or ethically perform experiments on society, as we can with physical objects. So the claims of social sciences (such as economics) to be scientific were a fraud. All economics could teach us was economic history. It could never predict the future. There were no scientific constants in society.

The reasoning behind this is that to describe the behaviour of physical objects, natural scientists need to focus on only a few key variables. A small number of equations are usually enough to predict them with tolerable accuracy. But we would need far more variables to describe even the simplest biological system; even more to describe complex systems like human beings; and a multitude to describe society, which is a complex arrangement of complex relationships between complex creatures. And many of those variables, like the motives and relationships between particular individuals, we can never actually know.

Though he originally shared this view, Hayek later came to accept that the trial and error methods of the natural sciences might have some relevance in the study of society, albeit a very limited one. He still believed that the structures of social life are necessarily very complex. Competition, for example, only works because large numbers of people are involved: any attempt to boil it down to something manageably simple would strip out exactly what makes it work. Social phenomena are necessarily *complex* phenomena. Any simple theory about them is bound to be inadequate. We could never predict, for example, exactly what any specific individual will buy and sell tomorrow, and at what price.

But we may be able to predict the broad *patterns* of such phenomena. Hayek likened it to the pattern on a carpet. You can see the pattern even if you do not know what colour any individual strand happens to be. And other people would recognise the pattern from your description, even if you did not tell them its size and hue. In society, likewise, we might be able to predict the pattern of events, but we can never predict the actions of individuals, nor predict specific events.

Hayek believed that this scientific pattern prediction, limited as it is, may still be valuable if it helps us explain what conditions might produce various patterns of social activity. Sadly, he did not specify where its limits lie. We cannot predict the actions of individuals, he said, only broad patterns of activity: but then how broad is broad? It is a question that still divides Austrian School thinkers.

Why intellectuals like socialism

Legitimate social scientists may well understand the limitations of their own subject, said Hayek. But there are many other people who are unwilling to accept these limits and who argue that our increasing scientific understanding now makes it possible for us to reconstruct society in the same way that natural scientists have reconstructed the material world.

In *The Intellectuals and Socialism*, Hayek argued that this view is particularly common among intellectuals – the "purveyors of second-hand ideas" such as journalists, teachers, commentators and politicians. Their reputation hinges on them being a little ahead of public and academic opinion: so they continually put forward new but mistaken theories. And because they are communicators, these errors quickly spread.

Such intellectuals, claimed Hayek, resent the boundaries that legitimate science imposes on their ideas. They prefer to earn attention and respect by advancing innovative utopian ideas for the wholesale reform of society.

Perhaps they simply do not understand the limits to social science. Perhaps they believe that better research will overcome them. Perhaps they choose to ignore them. Perhaps they believe that it must be perfectly possible for people of their obvious intelligence to redesign our social institutions for the better. Perhaps they imagine that, on account of their intelligence, it is they who (at last!) would be running things in this brave new world. Whatever the reason, concluded Hayek, they are consumed by socialist ideas and the mistaken belief that human society can be shaped to conform to their particular hierarchy of values.

Socialism and the young

Utopian social ideas are particularly attractive to the young, noted Hayek. The alternative – conservative – view is nothing like as thrilling. While a measure of conservatism may be essential to stability, it is hardly a social programme, he said. Its paternalist, nationalist and often mystical nature will never inspire the young or anyone else who wants to improve the world; and it relies on the same use of power to impose its values as does socialism.

"Conservatism, though a necessary element in any stable society, is not a social program; in its paternalistic, nationalistic, and power-adoring tendencies it is often closer to socialism than true liberalism; and with its traditionalistic, anti-intellectual, and often mystical propensities it will never, except in short periods of disillusionment, appeal to the young and all those others who believe that some changes are desirable if this world is to become a better place."

– F. A. Hayek, *The Road to Serfdom*

At first sight, liberalism looks no more inspiring. Its ambition is necessarily limited, since liberals hold that social institutions have a life of their own and do not respond happily to our efforts to redesign them. The liberal wants only to make sure those institutions are left free to work efficiently for the overall benefit of us all.

Nevertheless, Hayek maintained that liberals do have an attractive ideal to put forward – and, unlike the socialist ideal, a practical one. "We must make the building of a free society once more an intellectual adventure, a deed of courage," he wrote in *Studies in Philosophy, Politics and Economics*. Liberals need their own utopian programme, he insisted, a "truly liberal radicalism" which stands up to the powerful, which is visionary, which rises above the politics of the day, and which "challenges the ingenuity and imagination of our liveliest minds".

Those words were written in 1949. The fact that, today, billions of the world's population now enjoy at least some measure of social, political and economic freedom that was denied to them then, is in large measure a tribute to the intellect, radicalism and vision of Friedrich Hayek himself.

WHY SOCIALISM
WAS A MISTAKE

COMMUNISM WAS A significant world force for most of Hayek's life. Russia went communist when he was in his teens; only just before he died did the Soviet system there finally collapse. On the way, it inspired communist revolutions in China, Southeast Asia, Latin America and Africa, and imposed its power and doctrine on the countries of Eastern Europe. Even in liberal Britain and America during the interwar years and beyond, there was a feeling that, if not communism, then some form of state socialism and central economic planning was not only desirable but inevitable. Britain, Hayek's adopted home, went so far along this road in the 1940s as to create a welfare state and nationalise most of its key industries. Other European and Scandinavian states were not far behind.

The reality that confronted Hayek, then, was the widespread belief, throughout East and West, in large-scale central planning and control of industry. His challenge was to show that such planning could not match the effectiveness of the market order, and that such control posed a serious threat to human freedom.

Today, fewer people believe that the means of production – land, labour and industrial equipment – should be taken into state control, or directed by some central state planning agency. Many people therefore dismiss Hayek's critique as outdated, tilting at a target that no longer exists. But even if extreme socialist ideas have faded, Hayek's arguments remain very relevant. They apply to all forms of what he calls *collectivism* – any political outlook that gives groups and group objectives priority over individuals, including even moderate socialist control over resources.

Even moderate socialists suffer the same problem as the state central planner: that they simply cannot gather the information needed to make their interventions work, nor foresee the unintended consequences. To push through their vision, they still need to acquire power – and power corrupts. In *The Road to Serfdom*, Hayek explains how even democratic socialism may slide into the kind of repression that no democratic socialist actually wants.

Capitalism is not contradictory

Karl Marx, who gave communism its intellectual foundations, believed that capitalism's internal contradictions would ultimately destroy it. Competition requires firms to become more and more efficient. That, he argued, would force companies to grow in order to capture the efficiencies of larger-scale production. They would grow bigger and bigger, until the world was dominated by a few giant monopolies, focused on profit and caring little for the public. The only antidote would be intervention, planning and public control of industry.

Hayek accepted none of this analysis. He objected that larger firms are not always more efficient. Larger firms face higher administrative costs. Mass production might make their products cheaper, but it cannot serve minority tastes, nor respond quickly to changing conditions: smaller, innovative firms may well make a large manufacturer's entire product range obsolete.

And there is a big difference between size and power, Hayek stressed. Only firms themselves, through experience, can discover the optimal size within their market – not politicians or economists. It is true that in some industries, scale may well allow a firm to manufacture more cheaply than smaller ones. Breaking it up might simply mean higher prices and no benefit to the public. A firm might grow large, but its ability to abuse that position is limited by the fact that other firms could enter the market and take its business. So too could nimbler, smaller firms, who might eat into particular sections of its market.

The important thing, concluded Hayek, is that size should come from providing a good product that the public want to buy, and not from some special regulation or privilege granted by a political authority – so often the source of monopoly power.

Capitalism is not wasteful

Another argument for collectivist planning is that competition produces a wasteful diversity of different goods. Standardising these products into just a few, or perhaps only one, would bring efficiency gains and allow us to eliminate wasteful duplication and advertising.

This argument, insisted Hayek, completely ignores the fact that capitalism is a dynamic discovery process. Competing firms offer a variety of products, and customers choose the ones they think best. Competitors then try to see if they can improve on those products and give the public something they like even more. If they succeed, that then becomes the new benchmark for other people to improve upon. If we standardised production using today's products and technology, we would stop dead this vital testing process of the market and choke off all progress, leaving us yoked to technologies and products that would quickly become obsolete.

"It would clearly not be an improvement to build all houses exactly alike in order to create a perfect market for houses, and the same is true of most other fields where differences between the individual products prevent competition from ever being perfect."

– F. A. Hayek, *Individualism and Economic Order*

Complexity and planning

Some people argue that society has now become so complex that only central control can make it work. Hayek took precisely the opposite view: that our social and economic orders are so complex that they are completely beyond the capability of any planning agency to comprehend, let alone manage.

This takes us back to the problem of information. Through the price system, the market order processes and communicates a huge amount of information, much of it local, partial and personal, about where resources are most valued and in shortest supply. Central planners simply could not access most of this widely dispersed and personal information. They have no direct access to what people value. And to calculate how resources might best be used, they would need to know all of the possible sources, production processes and end uses for every commodity and product. Meanwhile, new uses are continually being discovered, new processes invented and new sources found or old ones running out. No central agency could possibly keep up with all this changing information.

If the planners could know all these things, then finding the optimal way of using our resources would, Hayek agreed, be no more than a computational problem. But the relevant information is dispersed between millions of individuals, with their own particular knowledge of their own changing local circumstances and their own changing needs and values. That sort of information simply cannot be collected, nor transmitted to a central agency before it is already out of date, nor expressed in a set of equations. What markets effortlessly process from instant to instant is in fact beyond the grasp of any conscious mind.

We are all planners

Some socialists argue that Hayek's picture of a central planning agency is just a caricature. They do not envisage a central agency trying to control everything; instead, a central authority would set the overall strategy for the group, leaving individuals and businesses at the local level to work within those guidelines.

But this 'indicative planning', said Hayek, forgets that we are all planners. We use our own local information to plan for what we think the future will hold. Nobody – not even a central planning agency – has perfect foresight, but on the basis of experience, individuals and firms become skilled at anticipating what others are planning, and at reconciling their own plans with that. This too is a valuable planning function, whereby people actively manage their use of resources, and do so skillfully, in such a way as to coordinate their activities with others who are doing the same management of their own.

"This is not a dispute about whether planning is to be done or not. It is a dispute as to whether planning is to be done centrally, by one authority for the whole economic system, or is to be divided among many individuals."

– F. A. Hayek, *Individualism and Economic Order*

This highly effective planning mechanism is exactly what the guiding plan would override, trusting instead to the wisdom of economists to plan for the whole group. That is reckless: as Hayek lamented, his profession had "made a mess of things". Furthermore, the requirement for everything to fit with the overall guiding plan would mean that all these individual private planners would always be taking their eye off prices – which contain the essential information needed for them to plan – and instead be trying to puzzle out whether and how their local actions would fit with the objectives of the general plan. So their ability to plan, manage and coordinate the use of resources locally would be reduced.

In other words, there is plenty of planning going on in a market order – and very expert and informed planning too. But it occurs at every point, among countless individuals and firms. Hayek warned that committing ourselves to a central plan, even an indicative one, means committing ourselves to only one large-scale guess about the future, rather than the many smaller-scale guesses of individuals in the marketplace. If the collectivist forecast is wrong, the damaging results will be large and widespread. But where individuals and firms are free to make their own forecasts, those predictions will be better informed by timely and local information; good guesses will eclipse the bad ones, and the damage done by wrong predictions will be more limited in effect and more quickly reversed.

"Is it really likely that a National Planning Office would have a better judgement of the number of cars, the number of generators, and the quantities of frozen foods we are likely to require in, say, five years, than Ford or General Motors, etc., and, even more important, would it even be desirable that various companies in an industry all act on the same guess?"

– F. A. Hayek, *New Studies in Philosophy, Politics, Economics and the History of Ideas*

The decline of democracy

To Hayek, indeed, one of the blessings of the free society is precisely that we do not all have to agree on one strategy for living. The market order is based on voluntary exchange – the fact that we all have different purposes, and can each gain from reciprocating them. Any form of planning, by contrast, presupposes some kind of shared purpose. But how can we get everyone to agree on a single purpose, when there are as many notions of the right goals for a society as there are individuals within it?

This is the problem that starts our journey down the road to serfdom, claimed Hayek. As politicians argue about what goals should be chosen, parliaments come to be seen as mere talking shops. Even if some goals can be decided, there will be more arguments about how best to achieve them.

Even if this was settled, too, no elected body is capable of undertaking all the detailed administration that is needed to put the whole economic programme into effect. Inevitably, decisions will have to be delegated to elected officials. And that gives officials a very dangerous amount of power.

In market orders, the overall outcome is what emerges when individuals follow general rules. Under collectivism, as Hayek explained in *Law, Legislation and Liberty*, the outcome is chosen in advance, and the efforts of each individual are marshalled towards achieving it. Plainly, this leaves the officials who are doing the marshaling with huge discretionary power to decide who should do what, where and when. Individuals are then no longer governed and protected by general rules that apply to everyone, the authorities included. Once officials taste such power, cautioned Hayek in *The Constitution of Liberty*, they "cannot be effectively controlled by democratic assemblies".

This is no mere scaremongering. Even in nominally free societies such as Britain and America, unelected officials have the power to make law in particular areas, and have wide discretion over how it is enforced. Hayek concluded that the "greatest danger to liberty today" came from such administrators, using their wide powers to achieve "what they regard as the public good".

Arbitrary treatment

A collectivist society cannot logically avoid this. If the planned outcome is to be achieved and not thwarted, the authorities must be able to direct the whole of the group's resources towards that end. They cannot leave the job up to the workings of general rules, nor be limited by such rules. But once the restraints on government power have been broken in this way, thought Hayek, none of us are safe from the arbitrary power of those in authority.

Some people still maintain that it is worth giving up a small measure of economic freedom in order to attain other things we value, such as the social aims of the collective vision. Not so, replied Hayek. The power to control economic resources is the power to control our lives. For example, where the state controls medical resources, it is no longer our decision whether some particular treatment is worth the cost. The authorities literally have the power of life and death over us. And if the authorities control the supply of paper, ink, printing, and room hire, communications and the media, how can objectors even protest at such decisions?

"To be controlled in our economic pursuits means to be . . . controlled in everything."

– F. A. Hayek, *The Road to Serfdom*

The problem of equality

Unfortunately, the collectivist authorities trap themselves in an impossible situation. Their efforts to replace or override the market order will never produce the promised abundance, only unintended and unwelcome results. To justify continuing with this strategy, then, the authorities have to turn instead to other arguments – such as the claim that it produces greater equality than does the market order.

But what kind of equality? It cannot produce equality before the law, observed Hayek, because in the collectivist, planned society, people and effort must be directed individually toward specific purposes by the authorities, rather than being guided and protected by general legal rules.

So can the collectivist society instead produce equality of wealth and income? Again, Hayek was sceptical. If the planners tried to set equal rewards for everyone, there would be widespread objections: many people would argue that they make an above-average contribution to social goals, and therefore deserve a larger reward. But allowing the authorities to set different rewards for different people gives them enormous discretionary power. Nor does it even end the arguments: indeed, there will be a constant tug-of-war between different groups, each insisting that they should be better rewarded.

The rise of dictators

The tasks facing a collectivist government are therefore enormous. It has to coordinate all government activities and to manage – or at least guide – how labour, land and other productive resources are used throughout the economy. It needs to identify and eliminate conflicts in the use of resources, and to make sure that those uses always fit with the aims of the plan. So vast are these tasks that, inevitably, representatives have to delegate them to unelected officials. Yet there will still be disputes, and disagreements that block decisions and action.

At this point, speculated Hayek, the public may well become utterly disillusioned with their politicians. They will demand stronger leadership. But if the jams are to be unblocked and arguments cut through, any such leader will need great strength of will – and few scruples. And once such ruthless leaders are armed with the vast power that is essential to running a collectivist state, restraining them may be difficult.

The suppression of truth

The moral qualities that come to be valued in a collectivist society, said Hayek, are quite unlike those of the liberal order. The people in a liberal society are free to behave as they choose, within certain minimal rules of conduct. The planned society requires individuals to do what the authorities determine is required for the achievement of its objectives.

That means objections and dissent must be suppressed. Individuals must expect to be uprooted and deployed at the direction of the authorities, since personal life now counts for nothing compared to the good of the collective – a good that is defined by those same authorities. In such a world, cruelty becomes almost a moral duty of the leader, said Hayek. You cannot make an omelette without breaking eggs.

But then you need to convince people, against the evidence, that the omelette is actually cooking. It will require propaganda to persuade people that present hardships are worth enduring in order to achieve the future benefits of the collective enterprise. Schools and the arts will be used to spread ideas of social solidarity, predicted Hayek. The lessons of history, law and economics must be re-written to demonstrate the superiority of the collective ideal. Information from abroad will have to be controlled. Conflicting ideas must be suppressed. But by then, mourned Hayek, rational discussion of social and economic events will have become impossible, and truth will no longer have meaning.

Attacking a straw man?

The Road to Serfdom did not stop Soviet communism marching through Eastern Europe and elsewhere, though it did make utopian social theorists in the West think again about the possible consequences of their collectivist ideas. It was not meant to explain the actual development of international socialism in Russia and national socialism in Germany, and the descent of those countries into totalitarianism; nor to suggest that every socialist experiment must end the same way. Rather, it made the more general case that collectivist ideas, if applied consistently, will tend to produce consequences that no socialist truly wants – and that the more consistently that socialism is applied, the worse the results are likely to be.

"Is there a greater tragedy imaginable than that, in our endeavour consciously to shape our future in accordance with high ideals, we should in fact unwittingly produce the very opposite of what we have been striving for?"

– **F. A. Hayek,** *The Road to Serfdom*

Nevertheless, it is the spectre of totalitarianism that haunts Hayek's critique of socialism in *The Road to Serfdom* and elsewhere, as indeed it haunted the world through much of his life – though many modern socialists regard this critique as beside the point. Hayek, they argue, saw collectivism only as something centrally planned, imposed and policed by the state. There are, they argue, many different forms of socialism, including varieties that are much less top-down, more rooted in popular acceptance, more spontaneous and more liberal than Hayek's straw man. "For thoughtful democratic socialists," wrote the American political writer Jesse Larner in 2008, "this line of attack is surely an amusing or infuriating distraction."

After all, he says, collective projects are perfectly compatible with individual freedom. People very often band together to create collective projects, with everyone involved – not some outside state authority – coming together to decide policy. Think of fishing cooperatives; fairtrade coffee collectives; workers buying out their factories; and even employee share ownership plans. This form of socialism, said Larner, "is not incompatible with democracy, markets, or liberty."

Hayek might answer that in a free society, individuals certainly have the right to group together and share effort and resources, and to decide for themselves how to run such projects. But individuals are free to leave a cooperative or collective if they do not like how it is working: they can join other groups, or give up on the whole idea and return to a non-collectivised sector. When, by contrast, socialism is applied consistently to an entire society, no such refuge remains, and people have no option but to comply with the collective view.

Computers or markets

Other critics have much more faith in the power of economic planning, and see Hayek's description of it as a gross caricature. American economist Allin Cottrell and computer scientist Paul Cockshott complained in 1994 that Hayek talks of state planning as if it were done by a single person. His description of the planning problem as "beyond the comprehension of any single mind" seems to underscore the point. But not even Stalin drew up all Soviet Russia's five-year plans himself. Planning would be the role of an organisation, not a person.

Furthermore, they said, the sort of knowledge that Hayek thought too dispersed to be centralised is now routinely centralised. Take his example of the shipper finding uses for empty cargo journeys – such vacancies are now posted and brokered online. Or think of today's online comparison sites. True, some knowledge is too fine to be centralised, but the local use of that knowledge need not prejudice the central plan.

Furthermore, while the market economy does indeed adjust to changing prices, reflecting relative scarcity of goods, the process is very slow: physical goods have to move before prices adjust, and it can take a long time for that to happen and for all its implications to work through the whole economic system. An array of supercomputers could do the job in a few minutes.

Hayek would retort that such criticisms are in fact a caricature of his own views. His point is more subtle: that the market system, paradoxically, makes use of far more information than anyone involved in it – or any agency – can actually grasp. That information is collected, processed, summarised and delivered to everyone who needs it through the price system, which is an information and processing network that spreads out into the entire market system and updates itself moment by moment. No agency, even one with many local offices, could ever collect and process so much information.

And while it is true that computers and the internet can now centralise and process much information that could not previously be collected, summarised and communicated to the centre fast enough to be acted on, that information is but a tiny part of what the market system processes. The key information that drives the market order is not information that is physical, public and organised, like the information that exists in ledgers and libraries. It is the inherently personal information of what people value; and it is producers' understanding of those values, their skill at reading changing market events, their knowledge of their own customers and their experience of how a particular market works. This information exists only in people's minds; it cannot be put into ledgers or equations any more than could an emotion or a prejudice. What does it matter how fast your computers work, if they do not have the necessary information to work on?

And is the market really so slow? Must goods move physically before prices can adjust? Hardly. One of the roles of speculators, brokers and agents is precisely to process and spread information quickly through the marketplace. Often, we know that a new product will be a smash hit or a dismal failure even before it hits the shops.

Does socialism erode rights?

Other critics remain unconvinced by Hayek's thesis that socialism is likely to erode democracy. On the contrary, they argue, Britain in the 1920s and 1940s experienced quite robust socialist governments, without its democracy being destroyed. Scandinavian countries remain democratic despite having socialist governments that take more than half the national income in tax. Indeed, claims the American economic historian Richard Tilman, civil liberties in the United States expanded fastest during Roosevelt's New Deal era, and again under the left-leaning administrations of John Kennedy and Lyndon Johnson. Democracy has proved more resilient than Hayek supposed.

Or has it? The share of the economy that is under the control of government has grown larger and larger in most developed

Western nations. More and more decisions are being made politically, rather than at the individual level. Western democracy seems powerless to check this drift toward collective decision-making. If anything, it promotes it: the more scope and power that a government has, the more will groups lobby for its favours, and the more electoral pressure there is on it to expand further. As the so-called Public Choice School economists remind us, this descent into populism must seriously erode the rights of individuals, unless prevented by very strong constitutional limits. But as Hayek himself noted, even the US constitution, often held up as a model, has not in fact proved able to protect the individual against the ravages of an expanding state. In *The Constitution of Liberty* and *Law, Legislation and Liberty*, Hayek gave a good deal of consideration to what kind of constitution might fare better at protecting the basic freedoms of a liberal order – as we shall see later in Chapter 9.

THE SOCIAL
JUSTICE MYTH

MANY PEOPLE WHO do not advocate collectivism or central planning or the stronger versions of socialism nevertheless call for greater 'fairness' or 'social justice'. Indeed, these ideas have penetrated deeply into the political debate in the West. But Hayek insisted that the term 'social justice' is vague and meaningless – and that the pursuit of this mirage undermines the institutions of a free society and prevents it from delivering its benefits to the public.

Two sorts of justice

Hayek maintained that there are two different uses of the word 'justice', and the confusion between them is responsible for much mischief.

The first use applies to what conduct we can expect from each other under general rules. If someone steals or breaches a contract, for example, we say they act unjustly, because the legal and moral rules that help us live peacefully together forbid such behaviour. It is important to note that justice in this sense applies only where people act deliberately and have a choice in the matter: if someone catches influenza, suffers bereavement, or has a physical disability, it may be unfortunate; but it is not unjust, because nobody has acted unjustly.

The second notion of justice, sometimes called 'distributive justice', is not about the rules of conduct between people, but about the distribution of resources between them. For example, people might argue that a more equal distribution of wealth or income would be 'fairer' or 'more just'.

Hayek contended that, in a free society, this second sense of justice – 'social justice' – is both misleading and meaningless. In the market order, the pattern of wealth or income is simply whatever outcome emerges as a result of everyone following general rules. It is not something that anybody deliberately chooses. It cannot be 'unjust' because nobody acted unjustly to produce it.

Social justice or freedom

True, said Hayek, we may not always like the distribution that emerges. Someone who works hard may still go bankrupt, another who is publicly loathed may still become rich. We might decry the 'injustice' of it all: but such complaints simply do not apply in a market order. Since the distribution is not due to the deliberate action of any individual or group, there cannot have been any injustice. An injustice is done only if someone deliberately breaks the rules of just conduct – say, by acting fraudulently. But there can be no injustice – and no justice either – in the distribution of wealth and income.

To achieve any specific distribution, moreover, we would have to jettison completely our existing rules of justice and morality, warned Hayek. People could no longer be left free to act as they choose, subject only to some parts of their conduct being restrained by general rules. Instead, they would have to be required to act in specified ways so as to achieve the chosen result. The present rules, which merely set limits on behaviour, would have to be abandoned because they would not produce the chosen outcome. And we are certainly not clever enough to produce a new code of justice and morality that would produce a particular social outcome – let alone one that everybody is content with. For example, how should we advise individuals to behave, in their daily lives, in order to be sure of producing an equal distribution of wealth?

Social justice and rewards

The fact that almost all politicians say they endorse 'social justice' does not make it valid or real, concluded Hayek – any more than a widespread belief in ghosts makes them real. The 'social justice' idea presumes that society acts deliberately: that society is a sort of person who decides the pattern of rewards – but it is not.

The mistaken view of society as a single person draws people into another mistake – that society has a single purpose. In fact, the reality is that people disagree greatly on what overall social outcomes would be desirable. Indeed, the only reason why 'social justice' can appeal to so many people, mused Hayek, is that it is so vague about what exact outcome is being advocated that the disagreements never come to light.

But when we try to flesh out what a 'socially just' distribution of rewards might look like, the impossibility of agreement becomes obvious. One thing most of us do agree on is that complete equality of incomes is *not* the right target, because then people would get the same rewards no matter how lazy or obstructive they choose to be. Plainly, reward must take effort or achievement into account. A common view, therefore, is that instead of complete equality, rewards should be allocated according to people's 'value to society'.

In a free society, said Hayek, this is an equally meaningless term. Who is to decide and measure what a person's 'value to society' is? Society is not a person, and has no values of its own. Only the individuals who comprise it have values, and those values are widely different and often conflict. One group of people might value the performance of a boxer, while others might appreciate that of a violin player; it is impossible to say which delivers the greater 'value to society' because the enjoyment of different groups cannot be compared. People cannot have 'value' to society because 'society' is not a being that values things.

Market rewards

How then to decide? People may complain of the 'injustice' of market rewards – that the pay of a dedicated and hard-working nurse, say, is a fraction of that of a bank executive. But consider the whole problem, said Hayek. How could we ever decide what would be the 'fair' pay of a nurse, or a butcher, a coal miner, a judge, a deep sea diver, a tax inspector, the inventor of a life-saving drug or a professor of mathematics? Appealing to 'social justice', he concluded, "does not give us the slightest help."

> "As soon as the state takes upon itself the task of planning the whole economic life, the problem of the due station of the different individuals and groups must indeed inevitably become the central political problem."
>
> – F. A. Hayek, *The Road to Serfdom*

Market rewards are actually a far better guide. People pay us for the goods and services we produce because they value those products. So market rewards do depend, in a very real sense, on the value that we deliver to other members of our society. They also reflect the scarcity and skill of the producers, the numbers of customers who want the service and the urgency or importance that buyers attach to it.

Market or merit

But market rewards do not reflect the moral and personal merits of producers, nor the time and effort they spend in bringing their goods and services to market. It does not matter whether their products required years of toil and investment, or were the result of a lucky accident. A fine voice or a ready wit are marketable capacities, valued by and well rewarded by others, even if the people who have them are odious creatures or make no great personal sacrifice in using these talents. All that counts is the enjoyment and value delivered to other people: competition, like justice, is no respecter of persons.

But, as with justice, that is no bad thing. There is simply no dispassionate and logical way of deciding the relative merit of different producers and how it should be rewarded. Merit is not a measurable quality: like beauty, it exists only in the eye of the beholder. Different people might have very different views on how commendable different qualities happen to be.

How do we even decide how much merit someone puts into what they produce? Should the merit of someone who invests years of toil but fails be rewarded, while another who brings value to millions be penalised because it was only a lucky accident? We do not actually want to encourage fruitless toil: economic progress is all about raising the value of what we produce and reducing the sacrifice that goes into it. Rewarding people for personal sacrifice would simply encourage personal sacrifice, not service to others. No economy could survive like that.

Power politics

Once a government tries to redistribute incomes on some basis of 'merit' or 'fairness' or 'value to society' or 'social justice', said Hayek, it will find itself being lobbied by many different groups, all claiming that they deserve more. Since there is no logical and dispassionate way to decide the issue, this pressure will lead to arbitrary and contradictory decisions. "Once politics becomes a tug-of-war for shares in the income pie," wrote Hayek in *The Political Order of a Free People*, "decent government is impossible."

The essential signaling function of the market is destroyed too. Hayek noted that some of the shrillest lobbyists are those industries that face a declining demand for their products, often because foreign suppliers are undercutting them. In the market, things would simply adjust: jobs and capital would gradually move away from those industries and into uses that were more profitable. But when 'social justice' dominates, governments will be pressured to maintain incomes in these industries, or grant them protection from competition. Every instance of such special treatment will encourage others to demand the same. Gradually the role of market realities in driving production and incomes will decline, and the role of political control will increase. Before long, incomes will no longer be decided by the value that producers deliver to their customers, but on their relative ability to lobby government. Rewards become not even a question of merit, but a matter of political influence.

This politicisation of rewards, thought Hayek, also drives nationalism. It is hard enough to determine how rewards should be distributed on the basis of 'social justice' in even a small community; it is completely impossible to do it for the whole world. And in any case, no country has the authority to impose its incomes policies on others. Groups who lobby governments to raise their own wages on grounds of 'social justice' are among the first, said Hayek, to resist similar claims from their foreign competitors. It is not just that such economic nationalism is distasteful; it also prevents markets working across frontiers, thwarting the peaceful economic collaboration of people across the world.

The importance of inequality

Inequality is not just the outcome of the market process: it *drives* the market process. The high gains made by successful producers act as a magnet, pulling people and resources to where the greatest value can be captured, and away from less productive and less valuable uses. So people and resources are attracted to where they will make the greatest possible contribution to future incomes. And this is a continuous, dynamic, growing process. The inequality that so many people resent is, in fact, the very attraction that steers effort and resources to their most productive applications, pulling up incomes at every level. It is the reason why incomes in the free world are so much higher than elsewhere, insisted Hayek. If we redistribute incomes in pursuit of equality, we block that magnetic force, and lose the future value, output and growth it could generate. This would not only make us in the developed world poorer; with growing populations dependent on the expansion of the global economy, it is the world's poorest who would suffer most. How can anyone call that 'social justice'?

As well as attracting emulators, the rich also have another important role in the market process: the essential role of testing new products. There are many things we could produce if we wanted to, but bringing new products to market is expensive and risky. New technology and set-up costs are high, producers cannot be sure that customers will want these new products, and the market is limited because the new products are expensive and customers may be unsure whether they are reliable and worth having.

But rich people *can* afford to take a chance on expensive new products. If they like them and tell their friends, the market widens and producers can increase volumes and reduce prices. If they do not like them, then producers will switch their effort and resources into more promising ventures. Successful products spread, unsuccessful ones are eliminated, and the luxuries of today become the commonplace objects of tomorrow, within the grasp of nearly everyone. No dynamic economic system could survive without this function, said Hayek: the reason that people today enjoy having cars, radios, refrigerators and air travel is because only a few years ago these were created as luxuries for the few. And it is only because we have rich, experimenting consumers that the horizons of the poorest have expanded so rapidly.

People with wealth and high incomes have other important social roles. They have the resources to experiment in creating new products and services, which expands choice and feeds the process of improvement. They can sponsor and rally support for arts, education and research projects that governments may neglect. And they can challenge an oppressive authority by propagating new political ideas that government officials might regard as deeply threatening.

Inheritance

Many advocates of 'social justice' are troubled by inheritance. Children should have an equal starting position at birth, they say; or at least, wealth should not be passed on to give children an unfair advantage.

An equal starting position, said Hayek, is clearly impossible. Only by equalising the wealth and income of all parents could we hope to equalise the position of all children at birth. Even then, there are many things to a person's upbringing besides money. Some parents are more intelligent, more caring or more skilled at child rearing than others. Parents pass on their particular moral and cultural values, as well as different mental and physical traits. And the locations and environments where children are raised can never be made identical. It is absurd to suggest we can 'equalise' such things.

Indeed, said Hayek, we should encourage the natural instincts of parents to equip their children to become good citizens and to make the most of their talents, since these traits benefit the whole society. And why should we resist parents' natural instincts to provide for them materially too? Parents passing on wealth helps avoid the dispersal of capital – which is essential for investment in new processes and products and encourages others to try to build up capital too. This benefits society just as much.

To Hayek, though, the key argument is that any such redistribution inevitably treats each person differently. The customary rules of morality and conduct, which apply equally to us all, must be torn up in order to achieve the specific overall vision. But it is upon these general rules that civilisation is founded.

Roots of the idea

Hayek believed that the dynamic nature of the market explains much of the attraction of the 'social justice' idea. Inevitably, changing events make some people better off and some worse, and the worst affected groups will be the loudest in calling for redistribution. Everyone sees the hardships of those whose wages fall; the wider benefits of a smoothly working market order are harder to observe. So governments are prompted to intervene in the name of the first at the expense of the second.

Another source of the idea is pure envy, though this is often camouflaged. Calls for redistribution are not always a disinterested appeal to help the less fortunate, but are often a case of special pleading by particular interest groups, suggested Hayek.

And most importantly, he continued, 'social justice' appeals to our deep-seated natural instincts that may well have been appropriate for the tens of thousands of years we lived in small face-to-face groups, but which are now entirely inappropriate for the global Great Society, where we can only coordinate our actions through general rules. Against such strong instincts, the acquired discipline of general rules will always struggle.

"I have come to feel strongly that the greatest service I can still render to my fellow men would be that I could make the speakers and writers among them thoroughly ashamed ever again to employ the term 'social justice'."

– F. A. Hayek, *The Mirage of Social Justice*

Criticisms of Hayek

Not surprisingly, Hayek's views on 'social justice' have caused great argument. For example, the American economist Theodore Burczak argues that the evolution of the social order is not as spontaneous and open as Hayek suggested. The moral and legal rules it is built on are themselves skewed by the values of those who happen to be judges and lawyers, rather than the values of ordinary people. And people cannot equally grasp the opportunities thrown up by financial and other markets. Hayek's idealism is therefore misplaced: this flawed system does not improve the life prospects of everyone. On the contrary, markets produce unnatural inequalities in wealth, income and opportunity. Burczak acknowledges Hayek's criticisms of state planning; but he proposes instead a sort of socialism in which privately owned companies are run by democratic workers' bodies, and governments redistribute incomes.

Other critics, including the Indian economist Amartya Sen and the American philosopher Martha Nussbaum, argue that the ability to choose, which is fundamental to Hayek's concept of a free society, means very little unless people do actually have the means to live and make choices. Unless we provide some essentials – like healthcare, education, a reasonable income and the ability to participate politically – choice is meaningless. A spontaneous order that allows people to starve to death hardly promotes the general welfare.

Burczak also rejects Hayek's view that agreement on the social objectives is impossible and that coercion would be required to pursue any collective goal. In fact we can and do largely agree on what constitutes 'the good life', he asserts. It may include, again, food, shelter, healthcare, education, and political rights. But there can be no 'good life' until the democratic system guarantees that these things are available to everyone. That means setting minimum levels for their provision, and engaging in redistribution in order to achieve them.

In reply to all this, Hayek might say that, though we share a notion of common decency, we do not in fact all agree on what kind of a society we want to live in – and certainly not on how to achieve it. The very fact that socialists and non-socialists argue about these things is ample evidence. But if there were anything less than total agreement, some people would have to be coerced into accepting the majority view, and some authority would have to be given power over them.

The great virtue of markets and the free society, according to Hayek, is precisely that we do not have to agree on the social outcome. Many different views and life strategies can coexist. Things need not descend into a fight over the spoils of economic progress, because varied markets serve many different tastes and competing demands. That variety allows experiment, progress and growth.

When debating different social systems, it is important to compare theory and theory, or experience and experience: to avoid comparing the theory of what one *might* achieve with the experience of what another actually *does*. In terms of the theoretical debate, Hayek has made his case. In terms of practical experience, Hayek might well argue that the more liberal societies have performed better than the more collectivist ones. In particular, the poor in free societies generally enjoy a much higher standard of living than those in collectivist societies: collectivism and redistribution do not in fact deliver the outcomes that their proponents aim at. Decades of socialism did not bring prosperity to Eastern Europe, India or China. Yet the growth of market orders in these places – even though greatly muted by government controls – in a short time raised a third of the world's population out of abject poverty.

THE FOUNDATIONS
OF A FREE SOCIETY

MUCH OF HAYEK'S work is an extended criticism of the collectivist thinking that dominated his age. But more positively, he also attempted to spell out what the institutions, constitution and government of a liberal order should look like. Some of these thoughts are in *The Road to Serfdom*, but they are spelled out more systematically in *The Constitution of Liberty* and in *Law, Legislation and Liberty*.

Liberalism means limited government

In Hayek's view, government does not exist to create a particular social outcome. That would be to impose the values of one group – even if it happens to be a majority – on others. But the majority could impose these values on others only though coercion – which is something we should seek to minimise. And our social order is the product of long and complex evolution: we do not properly understand how it works, so we would be unwise to grant anyone the power to try to redesign it wholesale.

For these reasons, a liberal government must be a *limited* government. We should not give our elected officials the power to do anything they want. That, warned Hayek, would create a serious risk to our freedom, security and standard of living. Rather, the role of government should be to *create the conditions* under which a peaceful and thriving social order might flourish.

To take an analogy, we cannot create a crystal by deliberately placing atoms one on the other; but if we create the right conditions, the atoms will do it for us, and arrange themselves into a crystal. Likewise, we cannot create a beneficial social order by deliberately trying to engineer it; government's role is rather to create the right conditions for it to emerge, by making sure that the rules of just conduct that produce it are upheld.

"Liberalism for this reason restricts deliberate control of the overall order of society to the enforcement of such general rules as are necessary for the formation of a spontaneous order, the details of which we cannot foresee."

– F. A. Hayek, *Rules and Order*

Unfortunately, Hayek believed, this judicial role of government has become eclipsed by its increasingly large role in running particular social projects. This has created serious confusion about the functions and appropriate powers of government, which has allowed the limits on authority to be eroded.

Two types of law

The trouble, said Hayek, is that there are two things that are both called 'law'. First, there are the general *rules of justice*, which enable a free society to function and flourish. Then there are the *administrative orders* that governments lay down to direct their own organisation of particular projects. Not only are these different; they may well conflict.

But the fact that both are concentrated in the same government hands is why even those countries that have sought to limit their governments through a constitutional separation of powers have failed in that aim. Little is achieved by separating powers that are themselves unlimited. The crucial thing is to understand the different powers that governments wield, and limit each as appropriate.

The first kind of law – the general rules of justice that are essential to the working of the social order – emerge in an evolutionary way, because they work and benefit those communities that adopt them. Such law cannot be *made*: it has to be *discovered*. Even the impressive legal codes written down by Solon of Athens or Hammurabi of Babylon, said Hayek, were not attempts to *invent* new rules of justice, but to *express more precisely* what the accepted rules were. And this kind of law *is* very commonly accepted. We follow the rules of justice, often without even thinking, because we have evolved and grown up with them and benefit from the peaceful social order that they create.

Certainly, disputes will arise as to what the exact rules are. Then it is the role of judges and the courts to ascertain that more precisely – defining the rules in more detail, resolving conflicts, and identifying how the rules apply in particular circumstances. But again, this judicial function of government is not about *making* law but about *discovering* and refining the accepted, general, abstract rules of conduct that will guide everyone, both now and in the future – at least until other rules evolve to replace them.

The second kind of law – which Hayek distinguished by calling it *legislation* – is the rules that government lays down to operate its own administration. When a government is empowered to marshal resources towards the achievement of some collective project, it needs to specify where and how those resources will be applied – what tasks civil servants must undertake, for example.

But it is not only government workers who are told what to do by this sort of law. Most projects will require taxes to be raised, so everyone will be affected. And if government gives itself powers to engage in new collective projects, the potential impact widens even further.

Creeping powers

Plainly, the government's administrative measures should be governed by the rules of justice. Unfortunately, the powers to define the rules of justice, to steer resources towards collective projects, and to decide what those projects should be, have all become concentrated in the same hands. This confusion has contributed to the growth and perversion of government powers.

First, the fact that all resolutions by elected assemblies are called 'law', said Hayek, gives administrative commands the false status of true laws – rules of justice – with the aura of general acceptance and respect this implies. Second, it suggests that the elected assembly has just as much authority to dictate the rules of justice as it does to dictate its administrative commands. This in turn suggests that legislators can replace the existing body of rules and re-shape society pretty much as they choose.

But when legislators do not see themselves as being bound by the rules of justice, or believe that justice is whatever they decide it is, there is no limit on their power, no restraint on the range and injustice of the commands they could issue in pursuit of their particular social vision. When governments believe they can 'run the country' just as they might run a factory, our lives and property become a mere input at their disposal.

"To leave the law in the hands of elective governors is like leaving the cat in charge of the cream jug – there soon won't be any, at least no law in the sense in which it limits the discretionary power of government."

– **F. A. Hayek, _The Political Order of a Free People_**

The dangers of democracy

Like other liberals, Hayek agreed that when collective decisions have to be made, they should be made democratically. But this does not mean that the majority should have unbridled powers to re-write the rules of justice and coerce the minority to their will. Even the most ardent democrat knows there must be limits on democracy – we do not give votes to children or foreigners, for example – and likewise if democracy is to deliver peace rather than tyranny, there have to be rules on how majority rule works and limits to what majorities can decide.

> "Democracy is essentially a means, a utilitarian device for safeguarding internal peace and individual freedom. As such it is by no means infallible or certain."
>
> – F. A. Hayek, *The Road to Serfdom*

A look at representative democracies confirms the point. The more power an elected assembly has to tax some groups and benefit others, said Hayek, the more it becomes a target for organised lobbying. Interest groups support and promote the particular politicians and parties who promise them benefits, and those politicians in turn promise benefits to enough interest groups to secure a majority. It is legalised corruption.

So the fact that an assembly is elected by a majority of the public does not mean that it should be free to pass whatever measures it sees fit. Without limits, the majority rule that helps secure peace may well become a threat to freedom and justice, and a means to oppress minorities.

Constitutional limits

This is why we have constitutions, which subject the elected assembly to a higher set of controls. They work through the separation of powers, by which some other, independent body judges whether the elected assembly's actions overstep those limits.

But most constitutions, Hayek believed, miss the target. The effective control of government power requires much more than a mere separation of powers. It requires the *rule of law*. All branches of government, he maintained, must act within general rules that apply to everyone; those rules should be known and certain; people must be treated equally under those rules; the judges who rule on them should be independent and non-political; and a private sphere of freedom and property must be protected.

Separation of powers has never worked, therefore, because elected assemblies have assumed the power to decide the rules of justice under which they operate. Even America's much-praised constitution, reflected Hayek, had failed to limit the growth of its government and the extent to which government could intrude into the private sphere of its citizens.

A model constitution

Separation of powers is certainly essential, said Hayek – but not in the sense of having two or more bodies with the same powers, especially if those powers confuse the authority to define the rules of justice with the authority to direct resources in pursuit of collective projects.

In Hayek's constitution, there would be two chambers of government, chosen in different ways and ruling on different sorts of issues. One would be charged with setting down the rules of just conduct – the general and abstract rules that limit the actions of everyone, including government itself. The other would be responsible for the organisation of government services; and though the range of functions it could undertake would not be defined, its powers and actions would be limited by the rules of justice laid down by the first body.

Hayek naturally wanted to make the first, rule-setting body as independent and non-political as possible. He suggested that this might be achieved by electing its members for long terms, after which they would not be eligible for re-election, but would assume honorific positions as lay judges. That means they would not be dependent on party support while in office nor concerned about their future afterwards. He suggested that they should be mature and able people, elected by their year group at, say, age 45 and serving for 15 years, creating an assembly of men and women aged 45–60 (still younger than in most present-day assemblies), one-fifteenth of which is replaced each year.

"[S]uch a system of election by the contemporaries . . . as a sort of prize awarded to 'the most successful member of the class', would come nearer to producing the ideal of the political theorists, a senate of the wise, than any system yet tried. It would certainly for the first time make possible a real separation of powers, a government under the law and an effective rule of law."

– F. A. Hayek, *New Studies in Philosophy, Politics, Economics and the History of Ideas*

A constitutional court might be needed in order to resolve conflicts between the two bodies, but Hayek believed that the distinction in their powers would be relatively clear.

Taxation provides an example of how the separation would work. Taxation is coercive, so the rule-making body would define the just principles under which taxes can be imposed – setting out general rules that apply equally to everyone. It would be up to the second body to decide how much tax should be raised, but it would be unable to skew the burden unjustly onto particular groups or minorities. So its members would be unable to elicit corrupting interest-group support for particular projects on the promise that other people would bear the costs.

The responsibilities of government

Within this constitutional framework, the responsibilities that Hayek saw for government were surprisingly broad. Its first duty, he maintained, is the security of its citizens – the provision of a defence force to protect against any threats from external powers.

In times of national emergency, that role would even extend to conscription: as a liberal, Hayek recognised the highly coercive nature of such forced military service, yet believed it could be justified in order to defuse even bigger coercive threats from outside. And ideally there should be the safeguard that any government demanding such service is itself limited by the rule of law.

The police, similarly, would have to have coercive powers to prevent citizens being coerced by others, and those police powers would also be constrained by general rules. But Hayek envisaged the government's protective role as much wider. It may have to organise responses to natural disasters such as storms, floods and earthquakes, he argued. Likewise the prevention of disasters such as fires and epidemics, or the rebuilding of social and market relations after them, might require compulsory powers to organise coordinated action, and the raising of taxes to finance it.

There are other 'public goods' that the market may not provide, said Hayek, largely because their benefit is general but is difficult to charge for. These include market information such as land registers, statistics and quality certification, plus certain roads and civic amenities where it is hard to charge those who benefit. But that is not to say that government should have a monopoly on providing these services, insisted Hayek. Although they may be financed through a compulsory levy, competitive firms could provide these services more effectively than civil servants.

Against progressive taxes

The size of a tax burden, said Hayek, is not the test of its legitimacy. The test is whether the coercion that is required to raise taxes is bound by general rules. Much of the mischief done by taxation is that it can be loaded disproportionately on particular groups, something which general rules would prevent.

The correct way to decide the size of the government sector, said Hayek, is to decide the size of the tax burden that people will willingly assent to – knowing that others will have to do the same – and only then decide how to spend it. Then the public sector is a matter of people each contributing to a common pool, from which they also draw services – unlike the present situation, where minorities are coerced into paying for the benefits of the majority.

Progressive income tax rates – whereby people on higher incomes pay higher rates of tax – fail the test of justice, Hayek believed, because they involve treating people differently. Progressive taxes are often advocated on the grounds of 'equal sacrifice' – that those on higher incomes feel taxes less. But, said Hayek, it is impossible to measure the 'sacrifice' that different people make, because we cannot compare how much pain different people feel when they are forced to give up part of their income. Also, in terms of incentives, the higher a person's income is, the more money it might take to spur them to effort – which might be an argument for regressive income taxes, but not progressive ones. And we should not underestimate the importance of incentives in a dynamic economic order: the signalling function of profits, which draws people and resources to their most productive applications, is muted when rewards are taxed away.

Monopolies of capital and labour

Another important economic role of government, contended Hayek, is to curb monopolies – of both capital and labour.

While he defended the right to associate, Hayek criticised the labour legislation in Britain and America that was in place at the time, observing that it gave unions important legal immunities and allowed them to coerce non-members into joining, or into complying with strike action. This coercive power might help to raise wages in unionised industries, but only at the expense of non-union workers – and of the unemployed, who would find it even harder to get work if employers were forced to pay higher wages.

Hayek's solution was to make all such restraints of trade illegal. Business cartels and similar schemes to thwart competition should be outlawed too. A *general* rule like this would be much more enforceable, and more just, than the present anti-trust legislation which leads to arbitrary decisions on particular cases.

Official restraints on trade are sometimes justified, said Hayek, but only if they are clear, general, and deliver an overwhelming benefit. Certification – doctors' qualifications, pure food laws, safety in theatres and suchlike – may be required, though government may not be the best agency to provide them. But we must avoid wage and price regulation of any kind (including rent controls): these restraints simply prevent the market from working and lead to shortages that then dislocate other markets too.

The welfare system

Hayek did not rule out government action to support needy groups such as people with disabilities, those incapable of work, orphans or the elderly. But again, rather than have discretionary rules for each group, he believed the best approach was a general minimum income guarantee, available to everyone as a safety net.

Hayek saw a case for compulsory insurance for healthcare, unemployment and pensions in order to prevent people becoming a charge on the welfare system. But he saw no reason why government should *provide* them, which inevitably would lead to the political manipulation of premiums. In fact, we want the market to price these risks. For example, if unemployment insurance were provided privately, then shrinking industries would face higher premiums. That would actually hasten their demise and speed the reallocation of resources into other sectors with better prospects.

Hayek also saw the case for compulsory basic education, so that all citizens have the basic knowledge and literacy they need to be effective members of society. But again, he did not believe the government should provide this. At most, the government should pay for basic schooling, through some mechanism such as education vouchers.

Criticism of Hayek

Given Hayek's general faith in the free social order to deliver benefits that we could not achieve ourselves by deliberate design – plus his warnings that socialism can easily slide into tyranny and his desire to minimise coercion – some people are surprised at the role and power he would allow government.

For example, the American libertarian economist Hans-Herman Hoppe says that it makes Hayek a social democrat rather than a liberal. Compulsory social insurance, the minimum income guarantee, subsidised education and other such programmes amount to a blank cheque drawn on taxpayers, since such 'minima' are invariably bid up through the system of majority rule. He finds it remarkable that Hayek was not concerned about setting any limit on the tax burden. And he is particularly alarmed at Hayek's endorsement of conscription: forcing people to risk their lives is about as coercive as it gets.

Hoppe thinks Hayek created a real problem for himself, because all this makes it hard for him to draw a line between a size and scope of government that leads to tyranny and one that does not. If government organisation of the military and police is acceptable, why not state pensions and education? And Hayek's proposal for a minimum income guarantee looks suspiciously like what the proponents of 'social justice' have been calling for.

In response, Hayek might have argued that he *had* held the line by ensuring that all government projects follow general rules that treat everyone equally. So they cannot be aimed to benefit particular groups, nor can their costs be loaded onto others – which is the main source of the exploitation that plagues government programmes today. And his constitutional structure should guarantee that equal treatment.

Another safeguard, he might have added, is that the volume of taxation would be decided in advance by the whole public; only then would the governmental assembly get to choose what programmes to fund from it. That two-stage process would tend to keep the tax burden, and therefore the growth of government, under control – in contrast to today, where new programmes are voted in one upon the other, and only gradually does the total cost become apparent.

Hayek also believed that this two-stage decision process, and the requirement for equal treatment of individuals under general rules, limits coercion. Individuals, he thought, will willingly sign up for a basic package of measures that they know is available to each of them should they need it, rather than being available to only a few favoured groups.

Is Hayek a conservative?

Though libertarians might see Hayek as a social democrat, he would still have seen himself as a liberal. But some critics have asked whether he was not, in fact, a conservative. After all, he argued that the existing social order encapsulated a great deal of 'wisdom' that we cannot replace with our own reason. And he specifically said that progress must be based within the tradition of our cultural inheritance. Does that not sound conservative?

At the end of *The Constitution of Liberty*, Hayek wrote a postscript entitled 'Why I am not a conservative'. His argument was that conservatives resist change, while he in fact wanted radical change: specifically, he wanted a lot more freedom than then existed in the world. And he wanted to change the direction we were going in, which was towards further and further curbs on freedom.

British policy analyst Madsen Pirie believes Hayek mistakes the nature of the conservative outlook. Conservatives, he says, are not averse to change – but like Hayek, they are highly averse to change being imposed on the social order by people in authority who think they know how to run things better. They do not wish to preserve the existing social and market orders, but to allow them to function smoothly and give them the freedom to change and develop – rather than having some preconceived outcome imposed.

Tradition and change are complementary forces in evolution.

Evolutionary change is rarely wholesale: instead, small changes that turn out to be beneficial are made within the existing wider framework. Massive change still happens; but it happens gradually, with the valuable features of the existing order being preserved. It is an outlook, says Pirie, that Hayek and conservatives both share.

THE CONTINUING
EVOLUTION

"**I**F ANY TWENTIETH-CENTURY economist was a Renaissance Man," reports the *Concise Encyclopaedia of Economics*, "it was Friedrich Hayek. He made fundamental contributions in political theory, psychology and economics. In a field in which the relevance of ideas is often eclipsed by expansions on an initial theory, many of his contributions are so remarkable that people still read them more than fifty years after they were written."

The claim is certainly true. People who knew Hayek speak of his extraordinary ability to penetrate right to the heart of a seemingly complex debate, making expert economists, social scientists, philosophers and psychologists stop and question their own fundamental assumptions. He did not have the quick and agile turn of phrase of Milton Friedman, that other great liberal economist who was his contemporary and friend. But Hayek had enormous wisdom, rooted in a lifetime of scholarship that was both broad and deep.

He was also the late twentieth century's most prominent and influential member of the Austrian School. Earlier in the century, the dominant Austrian thinker was Mises, who held that economic truth could be deduced from the very nature of human action. Hayek took a different view, seeing economic and social ideas as a matter of change and progress through trial and error. This took Hayek into his key insights – of markets, competition, morality and the law as *processes* by which we gradually discover the elements that build a prosperous and peaceful society; and of the fundamental limits to our own understanding of how this harmonious social order actually works.

"If we are to understand how society works, we must attempt to define the general nature and range of our ignorance concerning it."

– F. A. Hayek, *The Constitution of Liberty*

Naturally, such ideas have come under criticism, particularly in the years since the fall of Soviet communism, when their traction and relevance became more obvious to a wider number of people. Many libertarians, especially those in the Mises tradition, hold that Hayek's ideas and proposals are not sturdy enough to hold back the engulfing tide of big and intrusive government. Many socialists, by contrast, believe that Hayek overestimated the difficulty of assembling the facts needed to plan an economic system. But equally, there is now a growing body of libertarians who absorb Hayek's arguments and apply them to new problems; while some of the most interesting socialist thinkers are those who accept Hayek's revelation of the shortcomings of planning and instead propose more decentralised collective approaches.

Hayek's ideas, then, are not static or frozen in his time: they continue to stimulate some remarkably interesting and novel social thought. But that sort of evolution of ideas is how human beings make progress. Hayek himself would not have had it any other way.

FURTHER READING

This is not a full list of Hayek's writings, but an indication of titles that will be relatively accessible to the general reader.

Hayek on economics

Monetary Theory and the Trade Cycle (1929). Outlines Hayek's ideas on money, capital and business cycles, and critiques other theories.

Prices and Production (1931). Further development of the ideas of Hayek and Mises on money, credit, and the trade cycle.

A Tiger by the Tail: The Keynesian Legacy of Inflation (1972; revised edition 1978). Traces the roots of postwar inflation in Keynesian economic policies, which pressure government to expand and finance itself through inflation.

Choice in Currency (1976) and *Denationalisation of Money* (1976). Outline the idea of using competing private currencies as an alternative to inflation-prone government monopoly money.

Hayek on science and psychology

The Counter-Revolution of Science: Studies on the Abuse of Reason (1952). Argues that the attempt to apply the methods of the physical sciences to social issues produces a misplaced confidence in the ability of human beings to reconstruct their societies.

The Sensory Order: An Inquiry into the Foundations of Theoretical Psychology (1952). Argues that how the mind organises information shapes our perception of the world; the basis of Hayek's view of markets as a 'discovery procedure'.

Hayek on socialism

The Road to Serfdom (1944). Classic short wartime work, arguing that democratic socialism requires increasing central control that eventually leads to despotism.

The Fatal Conceit: The Errors of Socialism (1988). In three volumes, Hayek argues that socialism is based on factual and logical mistakes and that the belief that we can re-shape society as we choose is a catastrophic error.

Hayek on the liberal society

The Constitution of Liberty (1960). Classic statement of the intellectual ideas and principles of freedom that Hayek says have shaped and must continue to shape society, and proposals on how to re-establish a liberal society today.

Law, Legislation and Liberty: A New Statement of the Principles of Justice and Political Economy (3 vols, 1973, 1976, 1979). Restates the importance of a rule-driven 'spontaneous order', the inevitable dearth of information available to central planners, and a set of institutions for protecting freedom.

Knowledge, Evolution and Society (1983). Collection of four essays, encapsulating Hayek's views on the limits to human knowledge, the roots of a free social order and the evolutionary nature of society.

Hayek on ideas

Individualism and Economic Order (1948). Collects Hayek's ideas on the limits to our economic knowledge, the problems of socialism, competition as a dynamic process, and the false application of physical-science methods to society.

Studies in Philosophy, Politics and Economics (1967). Essays on topics including the theory of complex phenomena such as human societies, the rule-based nature of spontaneous order and the unintended consequences of human action.

New Studies in Philosophy, Politics, Economics and the History of Ideas (1978). More essays on the nature of human societies and economics, plus more tracing of the intellectual roots of the ideas of spontaneous order and freedom.

Materials about Hayek

The Essence of Hayek by Kurt R. Leube and Chiaki Nishiyama (1984). Essays providing an overview of Hayek's work in economics, political science, history and philosophy.

Hayek – his life and thought (1985). Video interview with John O'Sullivan in which Hayek outlines his principal ideas.

Hayek on the Fabric of Human Society, edited by Eamonn Butler and Madsen Pirie (1987). A leading journalist, philosopher, economist, historian and policy analyst each review Hayek's thoughts on the origin and nature of the social order. Contains the essay by Madsen Pirie, 'Why F. A. Hayek is a conservative'.

Hayek on Liberty, by John Gray (revised edition, 1998). Critical exposition of Hayek's belief that we are unable to know and understand our world, the importance of spontaneous order in enabling us to navigate it, and the concept of law and the limits to interventionism that this implies.

Hayek: A Tribute (1992). Video-biography of Hayek by the Adam Smith Institute.

Hayek: A Commemorative Album, by John Raybould (1998). Photo-biography of Hayek's life, ideas, writings and influence.

Friedrich Hayek: A Biography, by Alan O. Ebenstein (2001). Full biography of Hayek, his life, his extraordinarily diverse ideas and writings, and his legacy to political and economic science and human affairs.

Hayek's Challenge: An Intellectual Biography of F. A. Hayek, by Bruce Caldwell (2005). Large biography tracing the evolution of Hayek's thought, from the Austrian School influences on Hayek to his own development of individualist ideas in economics and social science.

INDEX

T

U

V

W

MILTON FRIEDMAN

by Eamonn Butler

Milton Friedman changed the world. From free markets in China to the flat taxes of Eastern Europe, from the debate on drugs to monetary policy, Friedman's skill for vivid argument and ideas led to robust and often successful challenges to a dizzying amount of received wisdom.

In this brand new guide, find out:

- how Friedman undermined Keynesianism and the prevailing wisdom of large-scale economic intervention
- how he demonstrated the true cause of the Great Depression and identified its real culprits (they weren't the ones jumping out of the windows)
- what Friedman believed really destroys the value of the money in your pocket and how it can be stopped
- his arguments for why regulations and minimum-wage laws actually achieve lower standards and greater poverty
- his reasons for why big corporations prefer markets that aren't free, and how high taxation harms the wealthy less than anyone else.

With more, too, on democracy, equality, global trade, education, public services and financial crises, this is a concise but comprehensive guide to the influence of a key 20th century thinker.

www.harriman-house.com/miltonfriedman